REST

GOD'S DESIGN
for
MANKIND

SATISH MYLAPORE

Trilogy Christian Publishers

A Wholly Owned Subsidiary of Trinity Broadcasting Network

2442 Michelle Drive

Tustin, CA 92780

For information, address Trilogy Christian Publishing

Rights Department, 2442 Michelle Drive, Tustin, CA 92780.

Trilogy Christian Publishing/ TBN and colophon are trademarks of Trinity Broadcasting Network.

For information about special discounts for bulk purchases, please contact Trilogy Christian Publishing.

Trilogy Disclaimer: The views and content expressed in this book are those of the author and may not necessarily reflect the views and doctrine of Trilogy Christian Publishing or the Trinity Broadcasting Network.

10 9 8 7 6 5 4 3 2 1

Library of Congress Cataloging-in-Publication Data is available.

ISBN 979-8-89333-426-5

ISBN 979-8-89333-427-2 (ebook)

DEDICATION:

I remember asking several questions about God to my mother, and I grew up seeking to know God personally. This is how my journey started, and now I find myself writing a book with the knowledge and wisdom He has given me. I thank God for His personal presence in my life, and I want to express gratitude to the people whom God brought into my life to transform me to where I am today.

- Thank you, Amma (Mom in my native language), for always trusting me and showing me unconditional love; your example sparked my initial thirst to seek God's love.

- Thanks to my aunts Raji, Vanaja, and Indu, through whom I first came to know about Jesus Christ in my life.

- Thanks to Allwyn, who offered me a different perspective about God, which changed my mindset to see God without fear.

- Thanks to God's ministers like Joseph Prince and Jesudian Silvester, through whom I began to see God as a loving Father.

- I am grateful to God for my children, Josiah and Josana, as they have enabled me to comprehend the heart of the Father each time I cherish moments with them.

- Lastly, but not least, thanks to my beloved wife, Sathya Priya, who has always believed in me and encouraged me to complete this book.

PREFACE:

Welcome to the pages of *"Rest - God's Design for Mankind."* As you embark on this journey with me, I want to offer you a glimpse into the heart of this book, its inspiration, and what you can expect to discover within these pages.

In our modern lives, characterized by the constant hum of technology and the demands of a fast-paced world, the concept of being at Rest has never been more relevant. Through the canvas of these passages, I invite you to explore the transformative power of knowing how God designed you (your original design by God) being at Rest—an understanding that has the potential to reshape how we engage with ourselves and the world around us.

The seeds of this book were sown during a time when I, like many of you, found myself caught in the throes of a never-ending race against the clock. The relentless pursuit of peace left me feeling disconnected from God and the moments that truly mattered. It was during one particularly introspective moment that I stumbled upon the profound wisdom of Rest, our design by God.

This book is not just a collection of words; it's an Exploration—an Exploration of the depths of the scriptures of God, an Exploration of the beauty that resides in each word, and an Exploration of the mysteries of Rest that are hidden in the Bible.

Within these pages, you will know who you are, how you are designed by God, God's intent to bring you into His Rest and His fellowship. This will help you find a holistic guide to weave Rest into the fabric of your daily life. Whether you're new to the scripture or seeking to deepen your understanding, my prayer/wish/assurance/hope is that you will discover scriptural insight.

As you read, I encourage you to bring an open heart and a curious mind. Allow yourself to absorb the words at your own pace, savoring each idea and integrating it into your unique journey. Whether you're flipping through these pages in search of tranquility, seeking to manage stress, or simply yearning to embrace the beauty of each passing moment, I hope you'll find what you're looking for.

Remember that Rest is not about leading a lazy life; it's about progress. It's about the small steps we take each day to honor the work of God in us. It's about learning to dance with life's rhythms rather than struggle against them.

Before we dive into the heart of the book, I extend my heartfelt gratitude to you for choosing to explore this path with me. May these words serve as a guide, a companion, and a source of inspiration as you navigate the journey towards a more restful and meaningful existence.

With gratitude,

Satish Mylapore

CONTENTS

PROLOGUE

Rest is one of the most beautiful traits that God has bestowed upon mankind. The common belief about Rest is that it occurs when a person is surrounded by peace, joy, and happiness while taking a moment away from work. However, these are the outcomes and fruits of being at Rest. In this modern age, people engage in various practices, medications, and even scientific research to understand how one can achieve a true state of Rest—to bring body and mind to complete peace. Some believe that riches and a luxurious lifestyle will bring this joy. The truth, however, is that these notions are far from reality, as they may provide only a fleeting sense of peace that fluctuates with circumstances.

Speaking of REST, I'm reminded of the words of a famous tennis player, who wrote, *"I had won Wimbledon twice before, once as the youngest player. I was wealthy, possessed all the material goods I needed—money, cars, and women, everything... I know it's a cliché, the same old story of movie and pop stars who tragically end their lives. They seemingly have everything, yet they are profoundly unhappy... I had no peace; I was like a puppet on a string."* Such a renowned star, who reached the pinnacle of success in his career and amassed wealth,

1

still couldn't find inner peace. This is because people often mistakenly believe that Rest is something to be pursued and inherited, whereas the scriptures offer a different perspective on Rest.

Matthew 11:28 (NKJV):

"Come to Me, all you who labor and are heavy laden, and I [Jesus Christ] will give you rest."

This scripture addresses two key points. First, it emphasizes that Rest is not something earned but rather freely given. Secondly, it underscores that true Rest is only found through Jesus Christ. This verse can be paraphrased without altering its original intent by stating, "He [Jesus] will grant you rest." What he bestows cannot be taken away, allowing you to enter into genuine Rest.

God originally designed this feature of Rest during creation. I pray that your eyes are opened to perceive the beauty of His wisdom, which has intricately woven Rest into every facet of human existence. I hope this enlightenment helps you grasp the true essence of Rest as depicted throughout the scriptures, revealing the exquisite nature of being at Rest. Our God is truly awe-inspiring, and His wisdom is unfathomable, as Romans 11:33 (MSG) aptly expresses, *"Have you ever come across anything quite like this extravagant generosity of God, this profound wisdom? It's beyond our comprehension; we'll never fully grasp it."*

His wisdom holds countless treasures hidden within such scriptures for thousands of years. However, God has now unveiled all things in Jesus Christ through His Holy Spirit, as stated in 1 Corinthians 2:10 (NKJV), *"But God has revealed them to us through His Spirit."*

God opened my eyes to perceive the design and significance of Rest in the initial chapters of Genesis between one and three. To better comprehend these scriptural mysteries, I've broken down the initial chapters of Genesis into smaller segments and presented various perspectives for examination.

1. **Creation - In the Beginning:** In this scripture, God reveals the path to salvation for mankind.

2. **The Fall of Mankind:** This passage discusses humanity's fall and its redemption through Jesus Christ.

3. **Creation and the Fall of Mankind – A Comparison:** This section aims to conduct a detailed comparative study between the creation

and fall of mankind, summarizing the significant losses humanity endured due to its fall.

Rest is a divine design of God, and understanding it may not come solely through the words of scripture; it may require deeper insight or even a personal encounter with God. Nevertheless, I firmly believe that the Holy Spirit's purpose is to guide you in comprehending the profound aspects of God's plan. I pray that the God of our Lord Jesus Christ, the Father of glory, may grant you the spirit of wisdom and revelation in the knowledge of Him. May the eyes of your understanding be enlightened, enabling you to discern and grasp the hidden mysteries of His Rest.

Proverbs 25:2 (NKJV):

> *"It is the glory of God to conceal a matter, But the glory of kings is to search out a matter."*

There is much goodness of God found in the scriptures, and it may take more than one's lifetime and even beyond imagination to understand all His goodness and love for us.

CHAPTER 1:

Creation – In the Beginning

Genesis chapters 1 and 2 describe the creation of the world, with some verses being easily understood and others often left pondered due to their complexity. Many times when we read these passages, we question whether there is any hidden truth within the creation verses recorded in the scriptures. One of the intriguing aspects that makes me reflect is the mention of night and day, darkness and light in the beginning. Several questions arise immediately:

Why did God include references to darkness and light during creation when we know that darkness does not represent God, as God is described as light with no darkness at all? Why not just have light and no darkness, and only day without nights? These questions lead to further pondering:

1. Why did God allow darkness to exist in the beginning of creation?

2. What was in God's heart when He created it?

3. What do these scriptures truly convey?

Certainly, there are more questions to explore. It is evident that these scripture verses were not randomly mentioned; there is undoubtedly profound meaning embedded within them. Let's begin by examining the very first verse of the Bible.

Genesis 1:1-2 (NKJV)

> *"¹ In the beginning God created the heavens and the earth. ² The earth was without form, and void; and darkness was on the face of the deep."*

An intriguing perspective emerges from these scriptures. It becomes evident that the word "darkness" appeared after the complete sentence describing the creation of heaven and earth. This suggests that darkness was not created but rather emerged on the surface of the deep earth. Darkness was not originally a part of God's creation plan; it simply appeared. This observation hints at something significant happening between the creation of heaven and earth and the appearance of darkness.

Consider these thoughts: God is not the source of darkness. It was not part of his creation. Yet, many have heard people attribute sickness or trials to God's actions, believing that He uses them to impart lessons or teach obedience. However, as the scriptures reveal, every good and perfect gift comes from above, descending from the Father of lights. Therefore, it is crucial to understand that it is not the Father's will for you to dwell in darkness, which biblically is associated with sickness, pain, and death. He desires to bless you beyond your wildest imagination.

Nonetheless, the question still lingers: "If God did not create darkness, then where did it come from, and why was it present?" If this question occupies your thoughts, that's excellent! We will address this question shortly. For now, let's hold onto the fact that darkness was not created but was discovered upon the face of the earth. Let us continue to explore further verses in the book of Genesis.

Genesis 1:3-5 (NKJV)

> "*3 Then God said, "Let there be light"; and there was light. 4 And God saw the light, that it was good; and God divided the light from the darkness. 5 God called the light Day, and the darkness He called Night. So the evening and the morning were the first day*"

You may have heard people say, "We have a season

to mourn and a season to rejoice, a season to be well and a season to have sickness." These sayings are also found in the book of Ecclesiastes in the Bible. However, when we turn to the verses in Genesis that proclaim, "God saw the light, and it was good," we discern that the presence of light symbolizes life and all the goodness it embodies. This revelation tells us that God takes delight in your life and well-being, not in your destruction and darkness, for it is not the will of our Father God that any should perish. God's intention has always been to care for you, to keep you safe and sound, and to bless you abundantly with goodness. God never intended for light and darkness to coexist. This becomes clearer when we observe how God separated light from darkness. This verse can also be understood as "separation from the light is darkness (or death)." Keep this thought in mind as we delve into a comparative study of these verses in the context of the fall of mankind.

Now, consider the last part of the verse closely where we find another fascinating concept when God declares, "So the evening and the morning were the first day." No, this isn't a mistake to call evening first. This pattern is repeated on the second day in Genesis 1:8, where evening marks the beginning of a full day, followed by daylight. In other words, darkness precedes or initiates a full day. This aligns interestingly with the Jewish calendar, where their day starts from nightfall, and their holidays, like Yom Kippur, begin at nightfall and continue until the next day's nightfall as one full day. However, as a common understanding, darkness symbolizes sin, death, and the power of Satan, while light represents God and life. This perspective can be referenced from the book of Acts.

Acts 26:17-18 (NKJV)

> *"17 I will deliver you from the Jewish people, as well as from the Gentiles, to whom I now send you, 18 to open their eyes, in order to turn them from darkness to light, and from the power of Satan to God, that they may receive forgiveness of sins and an inheritance among those who are sanctified by faith in Me."*

Looking at this verse diligently comprehends darkness to the power of Satan and light to God. This will probably intensify the question we have about the nightfall being at the beginning part of one full day... recollecting the other question, why did God even allow darkness?

I want you to note down all these questions so that, when we progress, we will be able to remember these questions and understand the context.

Questions:

- What does darkness mean?

- Why did God allow darkness?

- Was it in God's heart to have darkness from the beginning?

- If God did not create darkness, then why was it mentioned in the beginning?

- Why did God mention darkness/nightfall as the beginning part of the day?

Points Pondered:

- Darkness was not created but was found over the deep on the earth.

- Separation of light is darkness or death.

These questions and pondered points will serve as a foundation as we continue to explore and understand the context.

CHAPTER 2:

Fall of Mankind

When we examine the fall of mankind in the context of the book of Genesis, we often hear the explanation that Adam disobeyed God in the Garden of Eden, leading to his expulsion from the garden. While this perspective holds true, there's a deeper dimension to the fall. The most devastating loss for Adam was not just being separated from the garden but the severed relationship with God. This separation ushered in a cascade of consequences: sickness, hunger, and a world filled with pestilences, economic downturns, confusion, conflicts between individuals and nations, and ultimately, the relentless grip of death on humanity.

Over time, people's perception shifted, and they began attributing natural disasters like earthquakes and tsunamis to acts of God. However, it's essential to recognize that God is not in the business of causing destruction. As the scripture states in John 3:16 (NKJV), "For God so loved the world that He gave His only begotten Son, that whoever believes in Him should not perish but have everlasting life." God's primary desire is to offer eternal life and not to bring harm to His creation.

Choice:

Have you ever pondered why Adam disobeyed? It is because he had a choice to do anything, including the choice to disobey. Then why would God even keep choices for man and ask him to choose what is good, as it says in the scripture?

Deuteronomy 30:19 (NLT)

> *"19 Today I have given you the choice between life and death, between blessings and curses. Now I call on heaven and earth to witness the choice you make. Oh, that you would choose life, so that you and your descendants might live!"*

Why didn't God choose to allow only the things He approves of, eliminating the option for mankind to choose things that displease Him and avoiding the problem of separation from God? This would have simplified many matters, but God's thoughts are far higher than our own imaginations. Scripture explains that when God created all things in the beginning by His word, He chose a different approach for mankind. Instead of creating mankind as one of His creations spoken into existence, He intended to make mankind in His own image, endowing them with the capacity to make decisions and choose for themselves what is good. Even more significantly, God wanted them to have the ability to choose to fellowship with Him willingly.

As Psalm 139:14 proclaims, "I am fearfully and wonderfully made, Marvelous are Your works..."—this underscores the meticulous care and significance God placed into creating humanity. The Father, Son, and Holy Spirit share a profound fellowship within themselves, as evident in the Gospels where they consistently complement each other, reflecting a divine fellowship. God created humanity with the purpose of inviting them into this intimate relationship between the Father, Son, and Holy Spirit. However, God would not force anyone but desires that all come to Him through their own choices. This is why God made us in His image—to enable us to choose to have fellowship with God, which is life.

Yet, there remains a crucial point to consider. God is inherently holy according to His righteous standard. No one can have fellowship with God unless they possess God's own righteousness. Thus, God created humanity in His image, which encompasses His image of righteousness as well. Mankind could enter into the triune fellowship only by being righteous. This choice between "righteousness as a gift" and "righteousness earned through works" is symbolized by the Tree of Life and the Tree of Knowledge of Good and Evil. To fully grasp the meaning of these two choices, we need to delve deeper into the Tree of Life and the Tree of Knowledge of Good and Evil, along with the related scriptures.

Genesis 2:9 (NKJV)

> *"The tree of life was also in the midst of the garden, and the tree of the knowledge of good and evil."*

Genesis 2:16 (NKJV)

> *"And the Lord God commanded the man, saying, "Of every tree of the garden you may freely eat..."*

Options

Many teachings I have encountered in churches and books regarding the Tree of Life primarily relate to Jesus Christ, a belief I also share. However, I sought a deeper understanding of this concept directly from the scriptures and patiently waited on God to reveal more about the Tree of Life. My thirst for this understanding grew stronger with time, and one day, during my meditation, God opened my eyes to specific scriptures related to the Tree of Life.

Proverbs 11:30 (NIV)

> *"**The** fruit of the righteous is a tree of life, **and the one who is wise saves lives.**"*

Romans 5:17-18

> *"**For if, by the trespass of the one man, death reigned through that one man, how much more will those who receive God's abundant provision of grace and of the** gift of righteousness **reign in life through the one man, Jesus Christ! 18 Consequently, just as one trespass resulted in condemnation for all people, so also one** righteous act resulted in justification and life **for all people.**"*

As I contemplated these scriptures, I became captivated by their profound meaning, and the Holy Spirit illuminated my understanding of the Tree of Life. Consider Proverbs 11:30, where the scripture can be interpreted without altering its meaning to say, "The

Tree of Life is a fruit that comes from righteousness." Furthermore, reflecting on Romans, it becomes clear that the righteous act of one Man, Jesus Christ, results in "justification and life." Justification and life are depicted in the scripture as fruits arising from this one righteous act. Therefore, the "Tree of Life" can be likened to the "Justification and Life" that freely come through Jesus Christ.

In Genesis 2:16, God stated that man may eat of the fruit freely. So, what is life? If death signifies separation from God, similarly, life signifies fellowship with God.

Life = Fellowship with God

Putting together all these thoughts about the Tree of Life and providing as a summary, it might look like a mathematical equation; however, this will be simple to understand.

Proverbs 11:30—"The *fruit of the righteous is a tree of life*"

Replacing *fruit* of the righteous with "*justification and life*" (result of the work of Jesus Christ)

Replacing *life* with "*Fellowship with God*"

Replacing *justification* with *Pronounced Righteous* (justification in Greek concordance dikaiósis: the act of pronouncing righteous)

Hence, without harming Proverbs' scripture, we can write it as:

Fruit is "Tree of Life" which is *Justification* and *life*

Tree of Life is the fruit from one man's act (Jesus Christ), which is *"imparting righteousness* and *Fellowship with Father God"*

Righteous act of that one Man (Jesus Christ) results in *imparting righteousness* and *Fellowship with Father God"*

"Through the disobedience of one Man [Adam], death entered the world, and now, through one Man's righteous act [Jesus Christ], righteousness is freely given to all. Through this righteousness, the fruit of pronouncing righteousness and fellowship with God [Life] is received by all through Jesus Christ."

It effectively encapsulates the central theme of salvation and redemption through Jesus Christ as contrasted with the consequences of Adam's disobedience.

The term "knowledge of good and evil" is central to our discussion and, for simplicity, we will refer to it as the "Knowledge-Tree."

In Genesis 2:17 (NKJV), we find a well-known Bible scripture that is often taught to children in Sunday schools:

> *"17 but of the tree of the knowledge of good and evil you shall not eat, for on the day that you eat of it you shall surely die."*

At first glance, this scripture might make more sense if the tree were called the "tree of knowledge of evil," as it leads to death. In such a case, if Adam were to reach out to that tree, he would surely die because there is no understanding of goodness associated with it. However, the tree is named the "knowledge of good and evil," and yet, when mankind reaches for this tree, it still leads to death. This raises a fundamental question:

What does death mean?

In the scriptures, we learn that Adam lived for nine hundred and thirty years (930 years). However, God stated that on the day he eats from it, he shall surely die. Therefore, death, from God's perspective, is not solely the physical death that occurs when the spirit leaves the body. It encompasses a deeper meaning— getting separated from God and His fellowship. In this context, mankind could no longer have fellowship with God, marking a profound spiritual separation.

Death = Separated from God and His fellowship

How can mankind, who chooses to partake of the knowledge of good and evil, die when goodness is still a part of the knowledge?

In contrast to the Life-Tree, where righteousness is freely given, resulting in the fruit of imparted righteousness and fellowship with God (Life), the Knowledge-Tree lacks the gift of God. Here, mankind is given knowledge to discern what is good and evil, along with the choice to earn righteousness through this knowledge.

Romans 3:21 sheds light on this matter:

> *"But now the righteousness of God apart from the law is revealed."*

This scripture implies that there is a righteousness that mankind can earn through the Law, which differs from the righteousness given freely by God. The key distinction is that the righteousness from the Life-Tree is a gift that remains once received, bestowed by God Himself without retraction. On the other hand, righteousness obtained through the Law is not a gift but must be earned as wages by man, requiring continuous effort to maintain a righteous state. If one falls short, they lose their righteousness.

Upon partaking of the knowledge of good and evil, mankind is subject to the standards against which his righteousness is measured, which are embodied in the Law of God. The Law of God reflects the very character of God Himself. By eating the fruit of the Knowledge-Tree, mankind entered into a covenant with God to earn righteousness by adhering to God's Laws. It's important to note that the Laws were not necessarily given at the moment Adam ate from the Knowledge-Tree; rather, he came under the effect of the Law by partaking of the Knowledge-Tree. The period between Adam's consumption of the Knowledge-Tree's fruit and the giving of the Laws through Moses is akin to the period between infancy (nursing) and readiness for solid food.

In Jewish tradition, weaning signifies that a child has progressed beyond the fragile stage of infancy and can consume solid food instead of breastfeeding.

Weaning typically occurs between eighteen months and five years of age. Likewise, the period between Adam's act and the giving of the Law can be seen as the maturation phase (before weaning) during which the children of God were being prepared to embrace the Law, culminating in the delivery of the Ten Commandments through Moses.

God's suggestions

Have you ever wondered why God gave the law in the first place?

Romans 8:7-8 (NKJV) sheds some light on this question:

> *"7 For if that first covenant had been faultless, then no place would have been sought for a second. 8 Because finding fault with them, He says: 'Behold, the days are coming, says the Lord, when I will make a new covenant with the house of Israel and with the house of Judah—not according to the covenant that I made with their fathers in the day when I took them by the hand to lead them out of the land of Egypt.'"*

It is crucial to understand that it was not God's original intent to give the Law to mankind. Rather, it was mankind's choice to come under the Law in order to earn righteousness by fulfilling the righteous requirements of the Law. Thus, God found fault with the first covenant. However, it's important to note that when the scripture speaks of finding fault, it does not imply that God made a mistake by establishing the covenant and then regretted it. Instead, it reflects the choice that mankind had to make, and God respected it.

Mankind had two options:

Choose the Life-Tree, where God would make a covenant to keep you righteous as a gift and allow for fellowship.

OR

Choose to make a covenant with God, committing to keep all His laws and earn righteousness to attain fellowship.

Mankind ultimately chose the second option, thus creating the first covenant. In doing so, mankind chose to be separated from God, which is described as death. In other words, *God told Adam that by eating from the fruit of the Knowledge-Tree, he would be separated from God (death), and the only way to have fellowship with*

God (Life) would be to earn righteousness by adhering to God's standards (the Law).

What happened?

Now, let's delve into what happened to Adam when he ate the fruit from the Knowledge-Tree and how he became separated from God.

In Genesis 3:6-7 (NKJV), we read:

> *"...she took of its fruit and ate. She also gave to her husband with her, and he ate. 7 Then the eyes of both of them were opened, and they knew that they were naked; and they sewed fig leaves together and made themselves coverings."*

On the day Adam partook of the knowledge of good and evil, his eyes were opened, and from that very moment, he had choices to make—either to align with the standards of God, which are part of the "Knowledge of Good" and live, or to focus on his "Self," which is the "Knowledge of Evil," and transgress the goodness of God, resulting in separation and death. Here's a thought to ponder: Have you ever considered how humans are designed by God? One of the most precious insights the Holy Spirit revealed to me, albeit with a hint of humor, is related to the design and function of our eyes in our bodies. We can see and appreciate the beauty of the entire world, but we can never see ourselves to judge our own appearance. We were not created to fixate on our own beauty but rather to admire the beauty of others.

The first thing Adam and Eve did when their eyes were opened was to realize their nakedness. This passage in scripture indicates that they began to focus on their "Self." However, when God created them, He designed them to see and appreciate the beauty of others. For Adam, it was the beauty of his wife, the garden, the animals, the birds, and everything God created.

God always intended to design humans as dependent beings. Even in the book of Genesis, He mentioned, "It is not good that man should be alone," and thus created Eve. He didn't want them to be alone, so He blessed them with the command to be fruitful and multiply, imparting a generational blessing that encompasses family—the wholesome design of God.

Furthermore, Adam chose worldly things to cover his shame (nakedness), which he had become aware of. But God never intended for mankind to use worldly things to cover their nakedness. Instead, He crafted a tunic from the skin of a sacrificial animal to cover Adam and Eve. This act symbolizes the righteousness of God. The fig leaves that Adam initially chose represented his self-righteousness, as he believed it would grant him a right standing before God. However, a right standing before God could only be achieved through the shedding of blood and death. Therefore, a sacrificial animal was offered, and God fashioned a tunic from its skin to serve as a covering for Adam and Eve, signifying the righteousness of God.

Life = Fellowship with God

Death = Separated from God and His fellowship

Life and Death are choices given to mankind, and God suggests that Man choose Life, but Man chose Death

I've provided an illustrative representation of the fall of mankind to aid in understanding.

God Created Mankind of His Own Image

God   created   Mankind

Genesis 1:26 *"Let Us make man in Our image, according to Our likeness;"*

Tree of Life:	Tree of knowledge of Good and Evil:
Proverbs 11:30 *"The fruit of the righteous is a tree of life"* Genesis 2:16 *"Of every tree of the garden you may freely eat"* Romans 5:18 *"through one Man's righteous act the free gift came to all men, resulting in justification of life"*	Deuteronomy 30:15-16 *"I have set before you today life and good, death and evil, 16 in that I command you today to love the Lord your God, to walk in His ways, and to keep His commandments, His statutes, and His judgments, that you may live and multiply;"*

"Righteousness is a standard by which one can have fellowship with God."
1 John 3:10 *"Whoever does not practice righteousness is not of God"*

Righteousness as a gift   Righteousness to be earned

Tree of Life:	Tree of knowledge of Good and Evil:
Man can have fellowship with God by the righteousness** that is freely given to him. This righteousness leads to justification and life. **Romans 5:17 *"For if by the one man's offense death reigned through the one, much more those who receive abundance of grace and of the gift of righteousness will reign in life through the One, Jesus Christ."*	Man can have fellowship with God by righteousness** However, he needs to earn this righteousness by observing the virtue of God by law. **Romans 3:21 *"But now the righteousness of God apart from the law is revealed"*

Mankind chose the knowledge of good and evil

The first thing mankind did when his eyes were opened was he saw his "Self" being "Naked" and chose himself a covering from the fig tree. This is the beginning of the self-righteousness, the foundation of the knowledge of evil.

For mankind to have fellowship with God:

> He needs to abide to the righteous requirement of the law, which is the virtue of God. OR,

> He needs to be separated from the covenant of knowledge of good and evil so that he can have fellowship with God by the new covenant through the tree of life

CHAPTER 3:

Creation and Fall of Mankind – A Comparison

The Bible is composed of sixty-six books, with thirty-nine in the Old Testament and twenty-seven in the New Testament. It's essential to understand that the Holy Spirit inspired people to record these books in a specific order. While some incidents or stories in the Bible may not have occurred chronologically, the Holy Spirit guided their recording to provide edification. Not only are the books arranged in a specific order, but every scripture within them also serves to represent Jesus Christ and His works, showcasing the full demonstration of God's love for mankind.

Habakkuk 2:14 –

> *"For the earth will be filled with the knowledge of the glory of the Lord, as the waters cover the sea."*

I pray that God opens our eyes to see beautiful truths and the word of God (Jesus Christ) being unveiled within the scriptures and blesses you in all areas of your life.

When reading the scripture in Genesis, I observed that several elements have been sequentially recorded, providing an expanded understanding of the following aspects:

- The fallen state of mankind.
- God's eternal love for mankind.
- Redemption in Jesus Christ.

Let me illustrate this with an example, drawing an analogy from the lives of Abraham, Isaac, and Jacob:

Abram, who became Abraham, meaning "exalted father" to "Father of many nations," analogically represents the Father in Heaven, desiring to have children in His image.

Isaac, the son of Abraham, who was presented as a sacrifice by Abraham, symbolizes how Father God gave His only begotten Son, Jesus Christ, as a sacrifice for us and raised Him on the third day.

Jacob, the son of Isaac, whose name was changed to Israel by God, represents mankind being forgiven of their sins by God and transformed into new creations.

So, the sequence looks like this: Abraham -> Isaac -> Jacob (changed to Israel).

This parallels the progression of Father God (the Father of many nations) -> Jesus Christ (His beloved Son) -> Us (redeemed through Jesus Christ).

As I delved into these stories recorded in the scriptures, I discovered that the story of Joseph closely parallels the life of Jesus Christ, who was given as a sacrifice for us by Father God. The entire Genesis scriptures revolve around God's plan to redeem mankind from sin and death.

These mysteries led me to contemplate the meaning of the creation scriptures, and as I meditated, God revealed beautiful truths hidden even within the first few verses of Genesis.

Genesis 1:1 (NKJV)

> **"In the beginning God created the heavens and the earth."**

When I asked some believers where God is, I often heard the answer that God is in heaven. However, if we consider Genesis 1:1, it becomes apparent that heaven is a place created by God, implying that it may not have existed before His act of creation. While this idea may be challenging for some, the scriptural context supports the notion that heaven is a place created by God.

Genesis 1:1 tells us that after creating the heavens, the very next thing God created is the earth. In the context of the Bible, mankind is often symbolically referred to as "earth," "world," "dust," and so on. Earth, in this sense, is situated within the space that is described as heaven in the book of Genesis. Furthermore, God created all the places, animals, birds, and everything for mankind to enjoy and have dominion over before creating mankind itself. He placed mankind in the Garden of Eden, where we also find in the scriptures that God walked during the cool of the day to have fellowship with mankind.

Considering these scriptures, it becomes evident that heaven is a place created by God for the purpose of having fellowship with mankind, and "earth" represents mankind in the very first verse of Genesis. Thus, without distorting the scriptures, one could interpret the first verse as follows:

> *"In the beginning, God created the heavens (a place for fellowship with mankind) and the earth (representing mankind)."*

If you truly want to understand the heart of God, consider the very first message preached by Jesus in the book of Matthew: "Jesus began to preach and to

say, 'Repent, for the kingdom of heaven is at hand.'"
This initial proclamation by Jesus underscores God's
desire for humanity to regain a life of sweet fellowship
with Him. It reveals the profound extent of God's love
for us, a love beyond our imagination.

Genesis 1:2 (NKJV)

> *"The earth was without form, and void; and
> darkness was on the face of the deep..."*

In our study of the Fall of Mankind, we learned
that Adam chose to be separated from God, which
essentially resulted in his spiritual death. In other words,
God had forewarned Adam that on the day he ate from
the fruit of the Knowledge-Tree, he would be separated
from God, which equates to spiritual death. To regain
fellowship with God and attain life, Adam would have
to earn righteousness by keeping God's laws.

Moreover, the verse from John 3:19 (NKJV) sheds
light on this matter:

> *"And this is the condemnation, that the light has
> come into the world, and men loved darkness
> rather than light, because their deeds were evil."*
> *This verse underscores that mankind lived in
> darkness, and their actions were tainted by evil.
> This comparative study helps us understand the*

verse in Genesis where it describes Man as being "without form and void," signifying that all their deeds were evil, and darkness enveloped them both externally and internally.

Therefore, comprehending the creation and the fall of mankind reveals that it was not God's will for Man to dwell in darkness; instead, it was a choice made by Man.

Now, let's revisit the questions posed in the previous chapter, "Creation – In the Beginning," and consolidate them for reference.

1. What does this darkness mean?

"Darkness is the fallen state of mankind, where he is separated and deserted from the fellowship of God." This highlights the central concept you've explored regarding the consequences of mankind's choice to separate from God, resulting in a state of spiritual darkness.

2. Why did God allow darkness?
3. Was it God's heart to have darkness from the beginning?

God presented mankind with a choice: "Either choose the Life-Tree, where I will make a covenant with you to keep you righteous by giving it as a gift, and have fellowship, **OR** choose the Knowledge-Tree, where you (mankind) make a covenant with Me (God) to keep all my laws and earn righteousness so that you can have fellowship with Me (God)."

However, we know that mankind chose the Knowledge-Tree, which led to their separation from God. Hence, it was mankind's choice to be in darkness, and it was not the will of God.

4. If God did not create darkness, then why was it found in the beginning?

God did not create darkness, but man's decision to be separated *is darkness*.

5. Why did God mention darkness in the beginning?

The state in which man seeks to earn righteousness to have fellowship with God (Life) leads him into darkness, as it is written that no flesh shall be justified by the works of the Law. Since man chose this option, God described man's choice from the beginning.

6. Why did God mention darkness in the beginning?

As we saw in the fall of mankind, man chose first the covenant that separated him from God, which led into darkness rather than the other covenant which led him into light. The first choice of mankind to get separated from God is darkness then the light through redemption through Jesus Christ. This is the mystery that is hidden in the scriptures of night and day. Remember that.

This is so amazing to know how remarkably God has concealed the truths about the fall of mankind from the very beginning verses in the scriptures. This does not stop here; God does not stop to surprise us by His awesome wisdom. He not only concealed the truth about the fall of mankind but also hid the truth about mankind's redemption in Himself, and this can be seen in the very next verse in the book of Genesis.

Genesis 1:3 (NKJV)

"3 Then God said, "Let there be light."

As you look into this statement, it makes an impression that God commands light over the darkness, and in one perspective, this is correct. However, it is always good to see some of the scriptures in the original script. As we know, the original scripts were inspired by the Holy Spirit, and the translations have lost some of their meaning. The Old Testament was written in Hebrew, and the New Testament was written in Greek. Also, to further understand we will use Strong's Concordance to see how the same words are used differently in many places. In the year 1890, Dr. Strong published "Strong's Concordance"; the purpose of the Strong's Concordance is not to provide content or commentary about the Bible but to provide an index to the Bible. This allows the reader to find words where they appear in the Bible. This index allows a reader of the Bible to re-find a phrase or passage previously studied. It also lets the reader directly compare how the same word may be used elsewhere in the Bible.

In Hebrew, the words "Let there be" has the Strong's cross reference (Strong's Concordance number 1961) "Original Word: הָיָה," which is a verb and has meaning "Become or Be or Come to pass." This is the same word according to the Strong's Concordance used by God when he was talking to Moses from the burning bush.

Exodus 3:14 (CJB)

"14 God said to Moshe, "Ehyeh Asher Ehyeh [I am/will be what I am/will be]," and added, "Here is what to say to the people of Isra'el: 'Ehyeh [I Am or I Will Be] has sent me to you.'"

It's fascinating to see how the same word 'Ehyeh' (which is translated as 'I AM' in Exodus 3:14, according to Hebrew Strong's Concordance number 1961) is used in Genesis 1:3 *"Let there be* light." To clarify, let's consider an example: the word 'Rest' can be used in various forms, like 'Rest,' 'resting,' 'restful,' and 'rested,' yet they all convey the same concept of rest. With this in mind, we can rephrase the statement in Genesis by replacing "Let there be" with "I AM" without altering the scripture's meaning:

"I AM Light" (instead of Let there be Light)

This rephrased sentence immediately brings to mind the words of Jesus from the Gospel of John 8:12 (NKJV): "I AM the light of the world. He who follows Me shall not walk in darkness, but have the light of life."

This "I AM the light" statement reminds us of the redemption offered through Jesus Christ, the Light in our darkness.

God's wisdom is truly beautiful. In just the first three verses of the Bible, we can discern the creation, the fall of mankind, and God Himself as our Redeemer. Contemplating the awesomeness of our God and His omniscience fills my heart with joy and encourages me to trust Him wholeheartedly.

I've also created a visual representation to help illustrate how Jesus redeemed us from the curse of the Law.

God's eternal love on mankind

John 3:16 *"For God so loved the world that he gave his one and only Son, that whoever believes in him shall not perish but have eternal life."*

Jesus Christ – A fulfillment to restore mankind's fellowship with God

Romans 8:3-4 *"God did by sending His own Son in the likeness of sinful flesh, on account of sin: He condemned sin in the flesh, 4 that the righteous requirement of the law might be fulfilled in us who do not walk according to the flesh but according to the Spirit."*

Jesus Christ – Fulfillment of the law.

Matthew 5:17 *"Do not think that I came to destroy the Law or the Prophets. I did not come to destroy but to fulfill."*

We can see from the scriptures that both the law and the prophets have witnessed Jesus Christ. Romans 3:21 (NKJV) *"But now the righteousness of God apart from the law is revealed, being witnessed by the Law and the Prophets."* We can see this being fulfilled in Matthew 17: 3, *"And behold, Moses and Elijah appeared to them"* where Moses represents the Law and the Elijah represents the prophets. Matthew 17:5, *"This is My beloved Son, in whom I am well pleased. Hear Him!"*

Jesus Christ – Separated us from the Law

Galatians 3:13 *"Christ has redeemed us from the curse of the law, having become a curse for us (for it is written, "Cursed is everyone who hangs on a tree)."* Thus, Jesus separated us from the covenant of the knowledge of good and evil by his death.

Romans 10:4 *"Christ is the end of the law for righteousness to everyone who believes."*

Mankind a new Creation

2 Corinthians 5:17 *"if anyone is in Christ, he is a new creation; old things have passed away; behold, all things have become new"*

Now mankind is a new creation and
has been reconciled to God in Jesus Christ.

2 Corinthians 5:19 *"God was in Christ reconciling the world to Himself, not imputing their trespasses to them, and has committed to us the word of reconciliation"*

CHAPTER 4:

Effects of Mankind's Fall

The perspective of an ordinary person in today's world vividly illustrates the consequences of mankind's fall. The destruction we witness in this world, often misunderstood or attributed to "Acts of God," reflects humanity's blindness to God's Word. Our perception of "good" often differs from God's divine definition. We tend to link prosperity to personal effort, health to lifestyle choices, and wisdom to worldly knowledge. Many believe that success is attained through personal striving and the endurance of pain. However, God's economy operates on entirely different principles, beyond our human comprehension. All that humanity strives for is freely given by God, a demonstration of His goodness and favor declared from the beginning.

The destruction and the relentless striving we observe in this world are the fruits of the disobedience of the first man, Adam. Let's explore what mankind truly lost and identify the root cause of this loss.

"...it is sown a natural body, it is raised a spiritual body. There is a natural body, and there is a spiritual body. 45 And so it is written, 'The first man Adam became a living being.' The last Adam became a life-giving spirit"

As we delve into the separation of mankind from God, we realize that profound changes occurred both in the physical and spiritual realms at the moment of this separation.

Separation of Natural Body: The fellowship and communion between man and God in the beginning were akin to the joyful interaction between a loving father and his children. As a father myself, I cherish the moments spent playing with my two kids, going to great lengths to keep them happy and witnessing the genuine smiles on their faces. Moreover, I deeply appreciate the unique things they do and the way they speak, as these small gestures refresh my spirit and bring joy to my day.

This profound bond between God and mankind is beautifully illustrated in the book of Genesis. God entrusted Adam with the responsibility of naming all the animals and birds He had created. It was a delightful task that demonstrated God's trust and delight in mankind, resembling a father entrusting his possessions to his beloved son. God granted Adam dominion over all His earthly creations, much like a father granting authority over his possessions to his son. God took pleasure in observing the names Adam chose for each living creature. This joyful interaction epitomized the relationship between mankind and God during the time of creation.

However, this beautiful fellowship was disrupted by man's choice, resulting in his separation from God. This separation brought about significant consequences, affecting both the physical and spiritual aspects of humanity, as detailed in the subsequent verses of Genesis.

Genesis 3:23 (NKJV)

"Lord God sent him out of the garden of Eden to till the ground from which he was taken."

When mankind disobeyed God by eating from the tree of knowledge of good and evil, the consequences were significant. God, in response to their disobedience, drove them out of the fellowship they had enjoyed with Him in the Garden of Eden. This fellowship was a precious and free gift from God to mankind, characterized by close communion and intimacy. However, due to their disobedience, mankind lost this priceless gift, and they were expelled from the Garden.

The separation from God was not limited to the spiritual realm; it also had profound effects on the physical bodies of human beings. These consequences are detailed in the following verses of Genesis. The disobedience of Adam and Eve led to significant changes in their physical existence, as well as the world around them. This marked the beginning of a new chapter in human history, where they had to face the challenges and hardships of a world outside the Garden of Eden.

Genesis 3:7 (NKJV)

> *"7 Then the eyes of both of them were opened, and they knew that they were naked..."*

When man had fellowship with God, he was not mindful of himself, as his focus was on God. This was because God covered him with glory, as seen in the scriptures of Psalm 8:5 (YLT), which says, "...causest him to lack a little of Godhead, And with honor and majesty compassest him." He was surrounded by the glory of God, living in the way he was designed, and he could see only the glory of God surrounding him.

He never had a reason to look at himself.

However, the moment he ate from the Knowledge-Tree, his eyes were opened, and he saw himself, including his self-image, for the first time. This was because, at that moment, *he lost the glory that had surrounded him* and that God had provided to him freely. This marked mankind's first loss.

Genesis 3:10 (NKJV)

"I heard Your voice in the garden, and I was afraid because I was naked; and I hid myself."

Earlier, we observed that the relationship between God and Adam was akin to that of a father and child—a beautiful and loving relationship that God had established. However, when man lost his glory, he could no longer perceive God as his Father. Instead, he began to view God as exhibiting strange behavior, including condemnation, fear, and insecurity. This transformation occurred as a result of mankind losing the glory that once enveloped him, which God had freely provided. Consequently, condemnation, fear, and insecurity took root in the human heart.

This transformation underscores the significance of Jesus Christ reintroducing God to us as a Father.

It's remarkable because, even though God had chosen to refer to the Israelites as His children, the children of Israel preferred to use various other names for God rather than addressing Him as Father. While there is nothing wrong with invoking other names for our Creator, addressing God as Father instills a sense of personal and familial connection. This represents another loss suffered by mankind—*his inability to see God as his Father.*

Genesis 3:17 (NKJV)

> *"...the ground is cursed on your account; you will work hard to eat from it as long as you live."*

Genesis 3:19 (NKJV)

> *"You will eat bread by the sweat of your forehead till you return to the ground — for you were taken out of it: you are dust, and you will return to dust."*

God is eternal, and when He said, "Let us make mankind in our own image, according to our likeness; let them have dominion over the fish of the sea, over the birds of the air, and over the cattle, over all the earth and over every creeping thing that creeps on the earth," His intention was not for mankind to experience death. In fact, death was never part of His divine plan. Instead, His purpose was for mankind to enjoy His presence and have dominion over all His creation for eternity.

God created mankind to relish the joy of His presence and exercise authority over His magnificent creation forever. He blessed mankind with the command to be fruitful, multiply, and partake of the fruits and herbs of the ground as food without the need for toil. All humanity had to do was savor the fellowship with God, bask in His divine presence, and embrace His abundant blessings.

Unfortunately, mankind's disobedience led to a curse upon the ground. This curse compelled humanity to toil tirelessly for sustenance, and it condemned them to return to the dust from which they were formed. This curse represents mankind's physical separation from God. The ground, now cursed, ensures that the food man toils to cultivate ultimately leads to his return to the ground in death.

The food that you eat to live ensures to take you to where it came from; the food that came from ground takes you back to the ground; the bread that came from heaven (Jesus Christ) ensure that He takes you back to The Father.

Genesis 3:24 (NKJV)

"...He drove out the man; and He placed cherubim at the east of the garden of Eden, and a flaming sword which turned every way, to guard the way to the tree of life."

God placed the Tree of Life in the midst of the garden, allowing mankind to freely partake of its fruit. Symbolically, this tree represents the righteousness of God, given as a gift to humanity. This righteousness serves as the foundational requirement for fellowship with God. God's meticulous care in creating mankind is evident as the Holy Spirit records in the scriptures that we have been fearfully and wonderfully made, bearing the image of God Himself. He showered all His love on humanity, akin to a father's deep love for his child, with the ultimate goal of nurturing divine love and fellowship with humanity.

However, when mankind made the choice to seek their own righteousness, attempting to earn it by reaching out to the Knowledge-Tree, they lost access to the Tree of Life. This unfortunate decision led to their separation from God and the *loss of their cherished fellowship with The Father.*

Separation in Spirit: "Now faith is the substance

of things hoped for, the evidence of things not seen" (Hebrews 11:1, NKJV). It's important to recognize that mankind is primarily a spirit dwelling within a physical body on this earthly plane. This physical body was originally created by God with the intention that it would not decay or perish. God fashioned this body with great care and adorned it with His glory. However, when man fell away from God, this glory was lost, and the human body became susceptible to decay and mortality.

Genesis 2:7 (NKJV)

> *"7 And the Lord God formed man of the dust of the ground, and breathed into his nostrils the breath of life; and man became a living being."*

This scripture reveals that the spirit of God entered the body formed from the dust of the ground, transforming it into a living soul. In the original text, both "Breath" (Breath – Noun) and "Being" (Being – Noun) are nouns. Therefore, in context, they refer to a living thing or object. The Breath of God gave life to man, making him a spiritual being inhabiting a physical body. Consequently, when the glory of God was removed from mankind's body due to his transgression in reaching for the Knowledge-Tree, the body became susceptible to decay and death. It is the spirit within the body that sustains life. However, when the spirit of man also became separated from God, the body began to deteriorate and eventually die.

Genesis 5:5 (NKJV)

> *"So all the days that Adam lived were nine hundred and thirty years; and he died."*

Ecclesiastes 12:7 (NKJV)

> *"Then the dust will return to the earth as it was, And the spirit will return to God who gave it."*

When God told Adam, "In the day you eat of the fruit from the knowledge-tree you shall surely die," it does not mean that Adam would physically die on that very day. As rightly pointed out, Adam lived for nine hundred and thirty years before his physical death. However, the spiritual death occurred immediately when he ate from the forbidden tree. This spiritual death meant *separation from God's immediate presence and fellowship.*

Ecclesiastes 12:7 indeed highlights the separation of the physical body and the spirit. When a person dies, their physical body returns to the dust of the earth, while their spirit returns to God who gave it.

This verse emphasizes the separation of the physical and spiritual aspects of human existence.

Final Loss to mankind:

On the seventh day God brought all that he had created into his "*Rest.*" The last blessing you can see in the scriptures before mankind disobeyed and fell from God is that "Rest."

Summarizing the losses of mankind when he got separated from God (both physical and spiritual)

Beginning from:

"he lost the Rest to which God brought him"

"he lost his glory around him that God provided him freely"

"he started condemning himself as he could not see God anymore as his father"

"he had to toil for food and was cursed to be returned to dust from which he was taken"

"he lost his access to the life-tree and indeed lost the fellowship with God" "he got spiritually separated from God, but his spirit and soul, created by the breath of God, remained on the body that was created by God"

Hebrews 4:1 (NIV)

"Therefore, since the promise of entering his rest still stands, let us be careful that none of you be found to have fallen short of it."

We see clearly that mankind had miserably lost the root of God's heart of creating mankind: to bring him into His Rest. You may ask a question: How can you say that it was God's heart to bring everything into His Rest? Assurance of God's Rest will explain with all the scripture portions confirming that God's absolute interest was to bring mankind into His Rest for continued fellowship.

CHAPTER 5:

How Does "Creation & Fall" Relate to REST?

We have discussed the work of God from the beginning of this book, but it may be very bewildering to understand and relate these explanations to Rest. All these scriptures are even from the initial chapter from the book of Genesis, and they talk about Creation and Fall evidently.

REST in Creation: The exploration of Genesis chapters 1 and 2 delves into the creation narrative, focusing on the intriguing presence of darkness and light. It raises thought-provoking questions about why God included references to darkness when He is described as light. The discussion contemplates the significance of this and other questions:

The insight begins with the starting verse of Genesis, highlighting that darkness appeared after the creation of heaven and earth, hinting that it was not originally part of God's plan. It emphasizes that God is not the source of darkness and challenges the misconception of attributing sickness and trials to God's actions.

This part of the book talks about mankind falling into the darkness metaphorically, representing mankind falling from the design of REST God ordained for him and getting separated from the Father God.

Once this description is provided, the immediate next scriptures explain light separating from darkness, symbolizing life and goodness versus death. It asserts that God delights in life and well-being, desiring to bless us abundantly.

Loss of REST in Effects of the Fall of Mankind: The discussion explores the fall of mankind in the context of the book of Genesis, highlighting that Adam's disobedience led to not only his expulsion from the Garden of Eden but also the severed relationship with God, resulting in various consequences such as sickness, hunger, pestilences, economic challenges, conflicts, and physical death. The concept of choice is examined, which emphasizes the relationship through His grace or earned by the works of mankind.

This part of the book talks about mankind entering into death metaphorically, representing that mankind experiences spiritual and physical death, which is a result of falling away from REST (spiritual and physical REST).

CHAPTER 6:

Rest – Mysteriously Hidden in The Bible

It is very important for believers not only to know that God has brought us into that Rest which Adam lost. And we inherited this Rest through the finished work of Jesus Christ, not only to inherit but also to see, to know, to understand, and to enjoy the Rest God hid as a mystery in the bible, without which we will never be able to enjoy the fruit for which Christ died.

Rest in Temple of God

We are the temple of God

The word 'temple' comes from the Latin word 'Templum,' which means 'sacred precinct.' It is often described as a holy place, one that is connected with God or set apart for God's purposes, typically enclosed within walls. I once asked my non-believing friends why they go to a temple or place of worship. Their answers varied; some said they go to find peace, while others said it's to connect with God. There are various reasons and views from different people, as everyone in this world seeks a sacred place for their own reasons.

The temple is universally recognized as one of the holiest places, believed to be where the presence of God resides. However, God's ways are often different from what humans can think or imagine. You might be wondering what this means. Let's explore some scriptures from the Bible to shed light on this topic.

1 Corinthians 6:19-20 (NKJV) says, "Do you not know that your body is the temple of the Holy Spirit who is in you, whom you have from God?"

This is how our God has constructed His temple: You are His living temple, and His presence dwells within you as the Holy Spirit of God. Many people in the world still seek God's presence outside of themselves, diligently searching for it. They have zeal and fervently seek to enter into God's presence, often heading to man-made temples, believing they will find Rest. However, they lack the knowledge that whatever is built by humans cannot last forever, whereas what is built by God endures eternally.

John 2:19 (NKJV) records Jesus' words: "Jesus answered and said to them, 'Destroy this temple, and in three days I will raise it up.'"

God has masterfully built His temple through Jesus Christ. This temple was not constructed by humans, so there is no reason for doubt about entering into His Rest. In fact, God's pattern is to first bring us into His Rest and then have His Holy Spirit dwell in us, making us the temple of the living God.

As a believer, you do not need to wander in search of Rest. You simply need to realize that you have already been ushered into that Rest, and you can be sure of this because of Him. When you heard the word of truth, the good news of your salvation, and when you believed in Him, you were sealed with the Holy Spirit as a mark of ownership and protection by God. The Spirit serves as the guarantee of our inheritance in the Rest, which endures until the redemption of God's own possession, His believers, to the praise of His glory.

First tabernacle of God

After God brought the children of Israel from

Egypt, God called Moses and instructed him to build a tabernacle according to the patterns He revealed. The following scriptures describe the events immediately after Moses completed the construction of the tabernacle.

Exodus 40:34-38 (NKJV):

> *"34 Then the cloud covered the tabernacle of meeting, and the glory of the Lord filled the tabernacle. 35 Moses was unable to enter the tabernacle of meeting because the cloud rested above it, and the glory of the Lord filled the tabernacle. 36 Whenever the cloud was lifted from above the tabernacle, the children of Israel would proceed in their journeys. 37 But if the cloud did not lift, they would not journey until the day it was taken up. 38 For the cloud of the Lord was above the tabernacle by day, and there was fire over it by night, visible to all the house of Israel throughout all their journeys."*

There are two significant aspects to this scripture, occurring immediately after the completion of the tabernacle by Moses.

First, the glory of the Lord filled the tabernacle, signifying the presence of the Lord. Notably, when God provided instructions to Moses for building the tabernacle, He referred to it as the "tabernacle of meeting." This clearly reveals God's intention to create a place where humanity could meet with Him and enjoy fellowship. You might wonder how we can claim it was designed for fellowship. This tabernacle wasn't solely constructed for God to dwell among His children; it was also intended for fellowship and to provide acceptance to His children. This is evident because immediately after its completion, God called Moses and initiated communication from the tabernacle of meeting. He said, "Speak to the children of Israel, and say to them: 'When any one of you brings an offering to the Lord, you shall 'bring your offering of the livestock—of the herd and of the flock. 'If his offering is a burnt sacrifice of the herd, let him offer a male without blemish; he shall offer it of his own free will at the door of the tabernacle of meeting before the Lord. Then he shall put his hand on the head of the burnt offering, and it will be accepted on his behalf to make atonement for him." How beautiful is this love! A place was prepared for us to be accepted, where the Master of the universe, and the heaven of heavens, could not contain Him. Yet, He chose to dwell in the midst of mankind just to have fellowship and provide acceptance, as a father has with his children.

The second aspect mentioned in the scripture, immediately following the completion of the tabernacle of meeting, is as follows: "Whenever the cloud was lifted from above the tabernacle, the children of Israel would proceed in all their journeys. But if the cloud did not lift, they would not journey until the day it was taken up." In other words, this can be explained as the children of Israel rested whenever the presence of God rested on the tabernacle. When the presence of God was lifted from the tabernacle of meeting, the people began their journey. The presence of God consistently brought Rest to His people, and there was nothing that could take this Rest from His people, as He Himself was their Rest.

Building the Temple of God

David was the first man who had a strong desire to build a house for God. He had a passionate longing to construct a temple for the Lord. However, when he sought guidance from the Lord through the prophet Nathan, God's response was recorded in 2 Samuel 7:5-7 (NKJV): "Would you build a house for Me to dwell in? For I have not dwelt in a house since the time that I brought the children of Israel up from Egypt, even to this day, but have moved about in a tent and in a tabernacle. Wherever I have moved about with all the children of Israel, have I ever spoken a word to anyone from the tribes of

Israel, whom I commanded to shepherd My people Israel, saying, 'Why have you not built Me a house of cedar?'"

Furthermore, God said to David, "It was in your heart to build a temple for My name, and you did well that it was in your heart. Nevertheless, you shall not build the temple because you have shed much blood and have fought many wars. You are not to build a house for My Name, given the amount of bloodshed you have been involved in before Me."

The scriptures describe David as a man after God's own heart. Yet, when David earnestly desired to construct a house for God, God acknowledged his intentions and commended him for it. However, God also presented a reason why David wouldn't be the one to build the temple, citing his history as a warrior who had been involved in significant bloodshed that does not represent Rest.

It is very hard to digest when you see the perfection expected by God to even build a house for God. It is not even now about entering into the house of GOD but just about building it.

The Bible scripture below describes the essentials

before building a house for GOD.

1 Chronicles 22:9-10 (NKJV):

> *"9...you will have a son who will be a man of peace and rest, and I will give him rest from all his enemies on every side. His name will be Solomon, and I will grant Israel peace and quiet during his reign. 10 He is the one who will build a house for my Name. He will be my son, and I will be his father. And I will establish the throne of his kingdom over Israel forever."*

Who built the temple?

Solomon built the temple of God. What is the significance of Solomon building it? Solomon in Hebrew means peace; it is derived from the Hebrew word "shalom," which is *peace and rest*. God not only named him as peace, but God also promised that he shall be a *man of peace and rest* and will have *rest from all his enemies* from every side. Here, the effort of mankind was not mentioned to get into that Rest, but rather, God assured to give him that Rest; in other words, God would cause him to Rest before the temple of God was being built.

Where is it built?

> *"Then Solomon began to build the temple of the Lord in Jerusalem on Mount Moriah."*

Solomon built the temple of God in Jerusalem; the word "Jerusalem" means the "City of Peace" or "Foundation of Peace." Jerusalem was earlier named Salem, which is in Hebrew the root word of the name Solomon. Also, Salem is the place where the King Melchizedek (meaning King of Righteousness and King of Peace) met Abraham with bread and wine when he came after the war.

The Temple was built by a *Man of Peace and Rest (Solomon)*, where he had *Rest* from all nations around and built the temple in the "*City of Peace*" or "*Foundation of Peace*"—this is impossible to be incidental. Amazing wisdom of God is hidden in this scripture and is provided to us for our edification so we may understand the finished work of Jesus Christ that has brought us into this *Rest*, and this is our assurance!

It is very imperative to understand that the house of God cannot be built without man entering into this Rest.

Temple Blessings

Jesus, through His death on the cross and resurrection, has ushered you into His Rest. He has transformed you into the temple where the Living God can dwell. This truth is evident in the book of Acts. When the day of Pentecost arrived, the disciples were gathered in one accord in one place. Suddenly, a sound from heaven, like a rushing mighty wind, filled the entire house where they were assembled. Divided tongues of fire appeared, resting on each of them, and they were all filled with the Holy Spirit, enabling them to speak in other tongues as the Spirit prompted. The Holy Spirit of God now resides within you, and you have become the temple of the living God. This symbolizes that we are made the temple of the living God through Jesus, and the Holy Spirit resides into this temple, which makes it evident that Jesus Christ brought us into that *Rest* in his death and resurrection. Understanding this is crucial for every believer. But does it end here? No, God has initiated a new beginning for you to start enjoying His blessings.

God responds to the prayer of Solomon after dedicating the temple.

2 Chronicles 7:15-16 (NKJV)

"15 Now my eyes will be open and my ears attentive to the prayers offered in this place. 16 I have chosen and consecrated this temple so that my Name may be there forever. My eyes and my heart will always be there."

You are this temple because the Holy Spirit resides in you, hence the ears of the Lord are attentive to every prayer you make; the eye of the Lord is always on you not to find fault with you but to bless you and your going out and coming in; and the blessings of Abraham is now on you. His heart is now always on you to bless you and have compassion on you and, finally, to have fellowship with you, which Adam lost due to his choice.

As we read further on, the scripture shows how Solomon completes his prayer towards the temple of God, saying "Arise, O Lord God, to *Your resting place*." Yes, Solomon calls the temple as God's, as His own resting place, and now, so *are we His resting place*. This reminds us of the scripture of creation; the seventh day, God had finished the work He had been doing, so on the seventh day he rested from all His work.

Rest in the Laws

Every scripture is provided to help us understand the heart of God; otherwise, we could easily be led astray by our own assumptions. As mentioned earlier, the giving of the law is not the primary desire of God's heart, but He had to give it because of Adam's choice. God gave the Law to humanity, starting with the Ten Commandments, as a means to obey and inherit His blessings and fellowship. However, God concealed wisdom within these commandments and laws so that we may grasp the depths of our Father God's love for us and His longing to have fellowship with us.

Mankind's view about the Law

A common understanding regarding the laws of God in the scriptures is to obey the instructions provided in the scriptures. This is evident in passages like Exodus, where it is stated, "Now therefore, if you will indeed *obey* My voice and keep My covenant, then you shall be a special treasure to Me above all people; for all the earth is Mine. And you shall be to Me a kingdom of priests and a holy nation." Many people earnestly strive to follow all the laws laid out in the scriptures. However, the scripture also declares that all have sinned and fallen short of God's glory, and there is none who is righteous.

Different people, including Christians, seek to keep the law for various reasons. Some believe that by keeping the law, they can become righteous before God. Others do so out of fear of God's judgment and make earnest efforts to adhere to the law. Some keep the law in the belief that only by doing so will they be loved by God. There are numerous other reasons why people endeavor to keep the law.

Laws are a reflection of God's own virtue. However, it is essential to remember that humans are created in God's image. When the scripture refers to being made in God's image, it encompasses all the qualities of God. Adam was initially created with all these qualities, which included an inherent image of the law. He was called the Son of God, inheriting all of these qualities. However, due to his own choice in reaching out to the Knowledge-Tree, he became a spiritually bankrupt individual and lost the qualities God had intended for him.

John 1:12 (NKJV)

> *"But as many as received Him, to them He gave the right to become children of God, to those who believe in His name."*

God has provided His virtue as a standard, His

Law to help us realize that we have fallen short of His divine qualities, and without these qualities, we cannot have true fellowship with Him. However, many people still endeavor tirelessly to regain the image of these virtues, often not realizing that they cannot be earned through sheer effort. Instead, these virtues are bestowed upon us as a gift when we become children of God through inheritance.

Ten Commandments

The Ten Commandments mark the beginning of the giving of the Law, and this significant event occurred on the very first Pentecostal day after the children of Israel were liberated from Egypt. Historically, Jews continue to celebrate the giving of the Torah (Law) at Mount Sinai on the first Pentecost day. While it's a common Christian belief that the Law was given for us to obey, it's essential to delve deeper into the message that God has for us within the Ten Commandments. God, through His wisdom, has hidden His heart's message within these Commandments to reveal His perfect desire to love and have fellowship with us. The Ten Commandments can be grouped into three parts.

First part: First three commandments

3 "You shall have no other gods before Me.

4 "You shall not make for yourself a carved image—any likeness of anything that is in heaven above, or that is in the earth beneath, or that is in the water under the earth;

5 you shall not bow down to them nor serve them. For I, the Lord your God, am a jealous God, visiting the iniquity of the fathers upon the children to the third and fourth generations of those who hate Me,

6 but showing mercy to thousands, to those who love Me and keep My commandments.

7 "You shall not take the name of the Lord your God in vain, for the Lord will not hold him guiltless who takes His name in vain."

The first three commandments focus on our relationship with our sovereign God and heavenly Father. As I reflect on these commandments, it reminds me of my relationship with my own children. I am a father of two little kids, and I love them deeply, willing to do anything to nurture a loving and lasting relationship with them. However, I cannot imagine a scenario in which my children love or trust someone other than me.

God created humans as dependent beings. In the beginning, after God created Adam, He said that it was not good for man to be alone, so He created a helpmate for him. This act symbolizes our dependence on God. However, humanity often strays from God in their minds and thoughts, which is why God had to remind us of who He is to us and strive to restore our relationship with Him. God designed humans to have children to help us understand the heart of the Heavenly Father, and every earthly relationship serves as a reflection of our relationship with God.

These three commandments represent Relationship or Fellowship with the Father.

Second part: Commandment to Rest

Exodus 20:8-11 (NKJV)

8 "Remember the Sabbath day, to keep it holy.

9 Six days you shall labor and do all your work,

10 but the seventh day is the Sabbath of the Lord your God. In it you shall do no work: you, nor your son, nor your daughter, nor your male servant, nor your female servant, nor your cattle, nor your stranger who is within your gates.

11 For in six days the Lord made the heavens and the earth, the sea, and all that is in them, and rested the seventh day. Therefore the Lord blessed the Sabbath day and hallowed it."

Observing the Sabbath is established based on the seventh day of creation when God rested all that he created and is often seen as a crucial commandment, but it goes beyond merely abstaining from work. The Sabbath represents an opportunity for all of God's creation to enter into the Rest that God originally provided us in the beginning.

Sabbath day commandment represents entering into the Rest.

Third part: Moral Commandments

Exodus 20:12-17
(Providing shorter version instead of the entire passage)

Honor your father and your mother.

You shall not murder.

You shall not commit adultery.

You shall not steal.

You shall not bear false witness against your neighbor.

You shall not covet.

The rest of the commandments represent the inherent moral standards or virtue of mankind.

Ceremonial Laws

There are a total of 613 commandments (mitzvot) in traditional Jewish law, and these cover various aspects of life and conduct. These commandments include both moral and ceremonial laws. Many Christians interpret these laws, especially the ceremonial ones, as pointing to Jesus Christ or foreshadowing His work. This perspective sees Jesus as the fulfillment of the Old Testament law and prophecies.

For instance, the burnt offering in the Old Testament is often seen as a symbol or foreshadowing of Jesus Christ's sacrifice on the cross. The High Priest's role and actions in the temple are also seen as pointing to aspects of Christ's ministry and work.

This interpretation encourages believers to see Jesus Christ in every aspect of the Old Testament, showing the continuity between the Old and New Testaments and emphasizing how Jesus fulfilled the requirements of the Law. It underscores the idea that Jesus is the ultimate fulfillment of God's plan for redemption and reconciliation with humanity.

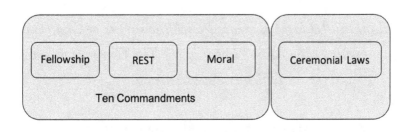

Adam in Ten Commandments

Adam is created in the image of God. Does this mean only by appearance? No. When the scripture says Adam is created in the image of God, it refers to the moment when God breathed the breath of life into his nostrils and he became a living being. This image encompasses not just physical appearance but also the qualities, virtues, righteousness (that of God as a gift), and everything that reflects God's nature. This is why Adam was called the Son of God.

To further understand this truth, consider that human beings can only reproduce other human beings. They cannot reproduce dogs, monkeys, or any other animal. Even within the animal kingdom, a dog cannot reproduce a monkey. This serves as an analogy of how man was created. When God created Adam in His own image and called him His Son, it signifies that Adam was created to reflect God in all aspects, both in nature and character.

Mankind (Adam) is created with the virtue of God, that points out to the Moral Laws of the Ten Commandments, which is Righteousness.

After creating Adam in His own image, the very first thing God did was to bring him and all that He created into His Rest (Genesis 2:2 for reference). After bringing mankind into His Rest, God placed them in a prepared location for fellowship with Him, which is the garden in the eastward part of Eden.

Adam is brought into His Rest, which again points to the Ten commandments.

Reading further into the scripture of Genesis chapter three, God walks in the garden during the cool of the day to have fellowship with mankind.

It is very evident that (Mankind) Adam had fellowship with God in the garden Eden, which is referred to as the Relationship with God in Ten Commandments.

Putting all this together, it is sufficient to say that when God provided the Ten Commandments to the children of Israel in Exodus chapter twenty, He did not give them new commandments but rather revealed the original state of humanity, the initial image in which they were created by God. This state was a gift to humanity, but Adam lost it due to his choices. Now, these commandments were given back to the children of God to pursue the original state (as a consequence of Adam's choice to eat from the Knowledge-Tree) so that they could be in fellowship with God. However, it is important to note that this state of righteousness cannot be earned but only received as a gift.

Mankind, through Adam, found themselves in a precarious situation where they were utterly lost because they were too weak to earn righteousness. Without righteousness, they could not enter into God's Rest, and without being in that Rest, they could not have fellowship with God. This is where the Ceremonial Law comes into play. Ceremonial laws served as a shadow, pointing to the Lord our Savior Jesus Christ and His works. Entering into His Rest is a crucial factor in enjoying a relationship with God, our Father.

The only commandment out of the ten to keep holy is
REST

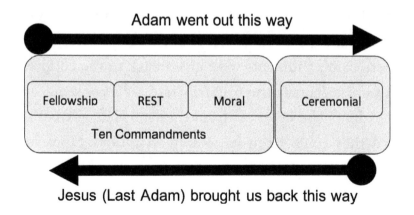

In the same route that Adam moved away from the Father, Jesus brought us back. Adam lost his relationship with God, and as a result, he could not experience the Rest that God originally brought him, leading to a loss of his moral values, which were inherent to his divine design. However, Jesus became our righteousness and restored us to the same state of Rest that the Father designed when He created Adam. This restoration makes us worthy of calling God "Abba Father."

Rest hidden in the Feasts of Israel

Scripture talks about several feasts celebrated by the children of Israel; some of them are weekly, others annually. Interestingly, these feasts are associated with Rest. In other words, there is no feast for a person if he does not Rest. Every feast in Israel is associated with the number seven, which represents the seventh day of Rest from God's creation or seven days of perfect creation; according to Jewish tradition, seven represents completeness or perfect peace, and finally, the seventh day is also celebrated as Sabbath. This is amazing to see how important God had made this kind of solemn Rest for mankind.

Let us delve into some of these Feasts, to understand their importance and how God had ordained them with Rest.

Weekly Feast:

Leviticus 23:3 (NKJV)

> *"Six days shall work be done, but the seventh day is a Sabbath of solemn rest, a holy convocation. You shall do no work on it; it is the Sabbath of the Lord in all your dwellings."*

Indeed, the Sabbath, observed every week on the seventh day, is considered a feast in the Scriptures. This designation highlights the significance of the Sabbath in reminding us of God's creation, which took place on seventh day. The Sabbath is a day of Rest, and it serves as a reminder of our fellowship and communion with God, drawing us into His Rest.

Yearly Feasts:

Feast of the unleavened Bread:

Exodus 13:6-8 (NKJV)

> *6 Seven days you shall eat unleavened bread, and on the seventh day there shall be a feast to the Lord. 7 Unleavened bread shall be eaten seven days. And no leavened bread shall be seen among you, nor shall leaven be seen among you in all your quarters. 8 And you shall tell your son in that day, saying, 'This is done because of what the Lord did for me when I came up from Egypt.'*

Every year children of Israel are not allowed to eat leaven during these seven days of the feast of the unleavened bread, but the Lord commands that the leaven shall not even be found in their house. This commandment is given by the Lord immediately after the Passover which points to the crucifixion of our Lord Jesus Christ. What do these seven days of unleavened bread mean?

This scripture from the Bible points out to the crucifixion of our Lord Jesus Christ, and His works have brought us back into those first seven perfect days. That means the work of Jesus Christ has brought us back into His Rest. The term leaven often refers to the sin, and our body refers to the house of God. Hence, by the perfect work of Jesus Christ, sin will never be found in the house of God, which means our body has been completely healed from sin. This is what the Lord had done to us when He had brought us out of spiritual Egypt. This is the reason the seventh day of the unleavened bread is not called feast of the children but called the Feast of the Lord. This shows how much He rejoices in bringing us back into His Rest, which even cost Him His own Son.

These two feasts from Jewish tradition serve to illustrate how God incorporated Rest within the Israelite festivals.

Why is it important to understand these mysteries?

God's wisdom in mysteriously hiding the revelation of Rest in the scriptures is profound and purposeful. By veiling this essential truth, He invites us to embark on a journey of discovery, deepening our understanding and appreciation of Rest.

Delving into the mysteries of Rest as presented in the Bible can have a profound impact on one's spiritual, emotional, and physical well-being. It provides guidance for living a balanced and purposeful life, deepening one's relationship with God and finding peace and meaning in the midst of life's challenges.

God communicates the importance of Rest through His commands, provision, care, and the rhythms He established in creation. Rest is an essential part of His divine design, intended for our physical, spiritual, and emotional well-being. By looking at the scripture in God's way of teaching, we can enjoy the Rest in Him and experience the blessings of His restorative grace, fellowship, and relationship.

Spiritual Revelation: God's wisdom in concealing Rest prompts us to seek Him diligently and delve into His Word. As we search for the hidden treasures of Rest within the scriptures, we develop a deeper intimacy with God and gain spiritual insight.

Personal Exploration: Hiding the concept of Rest challenges us to personally explore its meaning and significance. This active engagement fosters a sense of ownership and understanding that goes beyond mere information, leading to a transformative experience.

Divine Encounter: As we uncover the mysteries of rest in God's Word, we encounter Him in a more profound way. This divine encounter allows us to taste the Rest He offers and draws us closer to His heart.

Spiritual Growth: God's wisdom in veiling Rest encourages our spiritual growth. It requires us to meditate, pray, and seek wisdom, thereby maturing our faith and deepening our relationship with Him.

Revelation of His Character: The hidden nature of Rest reveals God's character as a loving Father who desires us to actively pursue Him and His gifts. It showcases His desire for us to engage with Him in a personal and meaningful way.

Appreciation of Rest: Uncovering the mystery of Rest helps us appreciate it more fully. When we comprehend the depth of God's Rest, we value it as a precious gift and recognize its impact on our lives.

God's wisdom in concealing the concept of Rest in the scriptures serves as an invitation for us to seek, explore, and encounter Him more deeply. It leads to spiritual growth, a richer understanding of His character, and a profound appreciation for the Rest He offers us.

CHAPTER 7:

Assurance of Rest

In the beginning, God created everything in six days, and Adam was created on the sixth day. Man enjoyed communion with God and was given dominion over all of God's creation.

Genesis 2:1-2 (NKJV)

> *"Thus the heavens and the earth, and all the host of them, were finished. 2 And on the seventh day God ended His work which He had done, and He rested on the seventh day from all His work which He had done. 3 Then God blessed the seventh day and sanctified it, because in it He rested from all His work which God had created and made."*

On the seventh day, God rested from all His works. So, the first day after Adam was created is the day when God rested all His works. In Jewish tradition, the number seven symbolizes completeness and perfection, both physically and spiritually. This marked the first day of mankind's fellowship with God, entering His Rest. This can be summarized as:

"God created everything and brought the entirety into HIS rest."

However, mankind miserably failed God's only command by eating from the fruit of the Knowledge-Tree, resulting in the loss of physical Rest and eternal Rest, which is experiencing God's life through the spirit.

Rest in the creation

A few important points to remember:

The Fall of mankind explains how humanity chose to be in darkness by partaking of the Knowledge-Tree. It also reveals that God Himself chose to be the redemption for humanity by becoming the Light.

Mysteries about Rest are also concealed in the creation account. In Jewish tradition, a full day is counted from sunset to sunset, signifying that a new day starts at night and is followed by the day. This illustrates that humans, along with all creatures, Rest at night and awaken refreshed in the morning.

To understand the context of Rest in terms of sleep, let's examine the following scripture:

Romans 6:11 (NKJV)

> *"Likewise, you also, reckon yourselves to be dead indeed to sin but alive to God in Christ Jesus our Lord."*

Let's replace some of the words in this scripture while maintaining the integrity of the text, supported by another scripture.

Dead is replaced with Sleeping

Matthew 9:24 (NKJV)

> *"He said to them, 'Make room, for the girl is not dead, but sleeping.'"*

These are the words of Jesus Christ, referring to a girl who was considered clinically dead but was, in fact, sleeping according to Jesus in spirit.

Sin is replaced with Darkness

John 3:19

> *"And this is the condemnation, that the light has come into the world, and men loved darkness rather than light because their deeds were evil."*

Psalm 51:4 (NKJV)

> *"Against You, You only, have I sinned and done this evil in Your sight."*

These verses in the scriptures help us understand that sin leads to evil, and evil is synonymous with darkness. Therefore, we can replace the word "sin" with "darkness."

Alive is replaced with Arise

Ephesians 5:14 (NKJV)

"Awake, you who sleep, Arise from the dead..."

Here, "Awake" and "Arise" convey the same meaning of rising up by the Lord.

Christ Jesus is replaced with Light (John 8:12: "I AM the light of the world")

Lord is replaced with Lord Christ Jesus

Now, with these word replacements, we can rephrase Romans 6:11 as:

> *"Likewise, you also, reckon yourselves to be sleeping indeed to darkness but arising to God in the Light of our Lord Christ Jesus."*

Now, let's explore the medical significance of sleep. (For detailed medical information, you can refer to the http://www.nhlbi.nih.gov/ website.) Below, I've provided some relevant information to help readers understand the importance of sleep.

Why Is Sleep Important?

Sleep plays a crucial role in maintaining good health and overall well-being throughout one's life. Adequate, high-quality sleep at appropriate times is essential for preserving mental and physical health, enhancing one's quality of life, and ensuring safety.

The quality of your waking hours is significantly influenced by the quality of your sleep. During sleep, your body engages in processes that support healthy brain function and the maintenance of physical health. In children and adolescents, sleep also contributes to growth and development.

Sleep deficiency can lead to immediate harm, such as accidents like car crashes, or it can have long-term effects on your health. Continuous sleep deprivation increases the risk of chronic health issues and can impact cognitive abilities, reaction times, work and learning performance, and interpersonal relationships.

Key Benefits of Sleep:

Healthy Brain Function and Emotional Well-Being: Sleep is vital for proper brain function. During sleep, the brain prepares for the day ahead by creating new pathways for learning and memory.

Physical Health: Sleep is crucial for physical health as well. The immune system relies on sleep to function effectively in defending the body against foreign substances. Prolonged sleep deficiency can weaken the immune response and make it harder to fight off common infections.

Daytime Performance and Safety: Quality sleep at appropriate times ensures optimal performance throughout the day. Individuals who lack sufficient sleep are less productive at work or school, experience delays in task completion, have slower reaction times, and are prone to making more mistakes.

Please note that this information provides a general overview of the importance of sleep for humans and is not exhaustive.

Note: This information about sleep is not very exhaustive but a gist about the importance of sleep for humans.

So, what are you trying to say?

You may be wondering why I'm emphasizing the importance of sleep. Sleep is a fundamental way our physical bodies Rest and renew themselves. Every human sleeps at night and when fatigued, as it is a crucial mechanism for physical restoration and the body's ability to combat diseases, which can be a factor leading to death. This arrangement is part of how God brings us into a state of Rest, which is essential for facing the challenges of life on Earth.

Matthew 13:10-11 (NKJV)

> **"10 And the disciples came and said to Him, 'Why do You speak to them in parables?' 11 He answered and said to them, 'Because it has been given to you to know the mysteries of the kingdom of heaven, but to them it has not been given.'"**

If you believe that all God intended is related to sleep, you may miss the deeper meaning. I am not advocating a lazy lifestyle or promoting laziness. Scriptures often describe how God conceals profound truths within simple aspects of the world. In Matthew's gospel, the disciples questioned why Jesus spoke in parables, to which He replied, "Because it has been given to you to know the mysteries of the kingdom of heaven, but to them it has not been given." God has a wonderful sense of humor in hiding His greatest gifts within humble things. Rest is indeed a valuable gift that rejuvenates our bodies, and God has placed it in the act of sleep. Similarly, fellowship with God is a precious gift hidden within the Rest.

1 Corinthians 1:27 (NKJV)

> *"But God has chosen the foolish things of the world to put to shame the wise, and God has chosen the weak things of the world to put to shame the things which are mighty;"*

Resting at night, during the dark hours, serves as an analogy for resting in God's presence to face any dark moments in your life. It is the solution to all the problems in your life, both physical and eternal. God's Rest can be understood from various perspectives, encompassing physical Rest as well as spiritual Rest for your spirit and soul.

Did you know? Sleeping at night is not a matter of personal choice but rather a tendency provided by God for the human body. Melatonin, a hormone secreted by the pineal gland in the brain, plays a crucial role in regulating sleep cycles, known as circadian rhythm.

Melatonin production is influenced by the detection of light and dark by the retina in the eye. When the retina senses light, melatonin production is inhibited, while it is stimulated in the absence of light. Special photoreceptor cells in the retina send signals to the suprachiasmatic nucleus in the hypothalamus, which then transmit these signals to the pineal gland. The pineal gland's production of melatonin peaks during nighttime hours, promoting physiological changes that support sleep, such as reduced body temperature and respiration rate. During the day, melatonin levels are low due to the abundance of light detected by the retina. This light-mediated inhibition of melatonin production is crucial for promoting wakefulness in the morning and maintaining alertness throughout the day.

Indeed, the wisdom of God is profound and beautiful. Despite mankind's choice to embrace darkness through disobedience, God's grace and love remain boundless. God uses simple elements of the world, such as sleep at night, to symbolize the Rest He offers to humanity to overcome spiritual darkness. It's a testament to His divine wisdom and His desire for our well-being and restoration to fellowship with Him.

"Likewise you also, reckon yourselves to be sleeping

indeed to darkness, but arise to God in Light our Lord Christ Jesus."

It's great that you're encouraging deeper exploration and understanding of the concept of Rest as presented in the Bible. Examining various stories, passages, and perspectives from the Bible on this topic can help shed light on its significance and implications for our lives.

Noah's Story of Rest

The story of Noah is one of the closest analogies of salvation through Jesus Christ. Noah is tenth descendant from Adam; during the time of Noah, the Lord saw the wickedness of man was great in the earth and that every intent of the thoughts of his heart was only evil continually. The Lord was sorry that He had made man on the earth, and He was grieved in His heart, so the Lord said, "I will destroy man whom I have created from the face of the earth, both man and beast, creeping thing and birds of the air, for I am sorry that I have made them." But, Noah was a just man, perfect in his generations, and he walked with God and found grace in the eyes of the Lord.

God came down to Noah and said to him that

"The end of all flesh has come before Me, for the earth is filled with violence through them; and behold, I will destroy them with the earth. Make yourself an ark according to the dimensions I give you." Noah built the ark according to God's command, and God brought all the clean and unclean animals to the ark to enter into it, and also God commanded Noah and his family to enter into the ark. Once everyone entered the ark, God shut the door of the ark and brought rain for forty days and nights that it became a flood and destroyed all flesh that moved on the earth: birds and cattle and beasts and every creeping thing that creeps on the earth, and every man. All in whose nostrils was the breath of the spirit of life, all that was on the dry land, died. Then God remembered Noah, his family, and every living thing in the ark and brought down the wind to dry the waters.

Genesis 8:4 (NKJV)

> *"Then the ark rested in the seventh month, the seventeenth day of the month, on the mountains of Ararat."*

Sometimes it is possible to overlook these details. Let's examine every part of this verse because it requires a profound insight into how the Holy Spirit has concealed a beautiful truth within it.

Ark: The ark symbolizes Jesus Christ (1 Peter 3:18-21, NKJV)

> *"18 For Christ also suffered once for sins, the just for the unjust, that He might bring us to God, being put to death in the flesh but made alive by the Spirit, 19 by whom also He went and preached to the spirits in prison, 20 who formerly were disobedient, when once the Divine longsuffering waited in the days of Noah, while the ark was being prepared, in which a few, that is, eight souls, were saved through water. 21 There is also an antitype which now saves us—baptism (not the removal of the filth of the flesh, but the answer of a good conscience toward God), through the resurrection of Jesus Christ."*

Seventh month: According to the Jews, the number seven represents the completeness and perfection, both physical and spiritual.

Seventeenth day of the month: According to Jewish symbolism, the number seventeen represents "overcoming the enemy" and "complete victory." It's worth noting that Jesus Christ achieved complete victory over death and the grave when the Holy Spirit resurrected Him near sunset on a Jewish month of Nisan 17. Additionally, it is believed that Noah's ark came to Rest on Mount Ararat on Nisan 17, which is the same day when Jesus returned to life.

Mountains of Ararat: Interestingly, the Hebrew word "Arar" means "Curse," and "Ararat" means "Curse is reversed."

Now applying the meaning of these on the verse of Genesis 8:4, it reads like this:

> *"Jesus Christ Rested perfectly (both bodily and spiritually) after overcoming the enemy (which is the death) with completely complete victory where the curse (over the mankind) is reversed"*

The perfect new beginning started when the ark rested on Mount Ararat, symbolizing the reversal of all the curses of mankind. This can be seen as an analogy to when Jesus Christ was crucified on Calvary. However, the Holy Spirit did not stop at this point in the story.

1 Peter 3:20 (NKJV)

> *"...in the days of Noah, while the ark was being prepared, in which a few, that is, eight souls, were saved through water."*

God spoke to Noah, saying, "Go out of the ark, you

and your wife, and your sons and your sons' wives with you." When they came out, there were eight people in Noah's family. In Jewish tradition, the number eight is considered to symbolize a new beginning. Scriptures also say that every male child born to a Jew is circumcised on the eighth day, as God instructed Abraham: "He who is eight days old among you shall be circumcised, every male child in your generations."

The judgment of God fell on the whole world, including the ark. However, we see that those eight people were also part of the judgment, but the judgment fell on the ark, which represents our Lord and Savior, Jesus Christ. The eight people survived God's judgment, while the rest of the world perished. This signifies that Jesus Christ became sin for us, took all our judgment on Himself, and gave us His righteousness, providing us with a new beginning and newness of life.

In the story of Noah, the new beginning started when the ark came to REST on Mount Ararat. This metaphorically represents how our new beginning started with the resurrection of Jesus Christ.

Jesus Rested - His death on the cross

I asked some of my Christian friends why Jesus came to this world, and the immediate answer I received was that all men have sinned and need a Savior who could save mankind from their sins. I agree with this, but the work of Jesus doesn't stop there. When Jesus lived in this world, He did many things, including:

- He revealed men's misunderstandings about God's infallible righteousness.

- Introduced God to us as a Father. Though God called Israel His son and children in many places in the scripture, the children of Israel never called Him Father.

- He came to reveal the heart of the Father.

- He came to fulfill all the scriptures.

- Yes, of course, He came to save mankind from sin.

This is by no means an exhaustive list, but it provides a few perspectives on the beautiful work of Jesus Christ. However, one of the last important things Jesus did before giving up His spirit was to bring us back into that "Rest" that mankind had lost.

"...he said, 'It hath been finished;' and having bowed the head, gave up the spirit"

Having bowed: The Greek word for "he bowed/ having bowed" is "κλίνας" (pronounced as "klinas," which also means "sleep"). This word is referred to in Strong's Concordance number 2827. According to the definition, it provides a meaning of "Rest."

Head: The Greek word for "head" is "κεφαλὴν," which is pronounced as "kephalēn." This word is also defined as "cornerstone, uniting two walls; head, ruler, lord."

Reading the scripture with these definitions in mind, the original scripture reads as follows:

"He said, 'It hath been finished,' and having rested the head, gave up the spirit." Jesus Christ rested His head, signifying that He had accomplished everything on earth. As a man, He stepped into the Rest that Adam lost. This is in line with what the scripture says in Colossians 1:18 (NKJV): "He is the head of the body, the church." As the body of Jesus Christ, we, the church, have also been brought into the same Rest through His finished work.

Rest in Genealogy

It may sometimes be challenging to grasp the significance of Rest; it appears to be such a simple concept. Did God truly plan and design this kind of Rest for mankind? The truth is that mankind entering this perfect Rest is not a simple matter; it came at a great cost, requiring the sacrifice of God's own Son to bring us back into His Rest so that we can fully embrace and enjoy His love.

Did God intend to restore this Rest to mankind through Jesus Christ, His only Son? Yes, let's explore the book of Genesis, where the names of the patriarchs from Adam to Noah, spanning ten generations, provide insight into how God, in His wisdom, concealed the message of the gospel in the scriptures from the very beginning.

In Genesis 5, this chapter offers the genealogy from Adam to Noah. Every Hebrew name is associated with a particular meaning. Jews believe in the power of words that come from the mouth, so they name a child based on the blessings they wish to bestow upon them. Whenever they call the child by their name, it serves as a reminder of the blessing associated with that name. The table below provides the names in both Hebrew and English, along with their meanings, in the same order as they appear in the scripture.

Hebrew Names found in the scriptures in Genesis 5	Meaning of the Hebrew name in English
Adam	Man
Seth	Appointed
Enosh	Mortal
Kenan	Sorrow
Mahalalel	The Blessed God
Jared	Shall come down
Enoch	Teaching
Methuselah	His death shall bring
Lamech	Powerful/Wild
Noah	*Rest*

Putting together all the English words reads as:

"Man Appointed for Mortal Sorrow, The Blessed God Shall come down Teaching. His Death shall bring a Powerful Rest."

Absolutely, it's truly amazing how God's wisdom and plan are woven into the fabric of creation and revealed through His Word. We can only be in awe of His divine design. Let us continue to seek and appreciate the depths of His truth and the beauty of His revelations. Amen!

What does this Assurance of Rest mean?

God's assurances of His Rest in the scriptures are intended to help us be sure of His Rest by providing unchanging promises, historical and prophetic evidence, fulfillment in Christ, and personal encounters with His presence. These assurances strengthen our faith and enable us to Rest securely in His loving embrace. His Rest in the scriptures helps us be sure of His Rest in several significant ways.

Unchanging Promises: God's promises of Rest in the scriptures are unwavering and unchanging. They stand as a firm foundation on which we can confidently build our trust. Knowing that God's word endures forever, we can be sure of the Rest He offers.

Divine Covenant: God often establishes covenants or agreements with His people, promising them Rest as part of the covenant. These covenants are sealed with God's faithfulness, making His Rest a guaranteed outcome for those who believe.

Tested and Proven: God's Rest has been tested and proven by countless believers who have found solace, peace, and refreshment in Him. Their experiences affirm the reality of God's Rest and encourage us to seek it with confidence.

Consistency of God's Word: The consistency of God's promises throughout the scriptures reinforces our confidence in His Rest. When we observe the same message of Rest echoed from Genesis to Revelation, we can be sure that it is a central theme of God's plan for humanity.

Peace Amid Trials: Experiencing God's Rest in the midst of life's trials and challenges provides concrete evidence of His faithfulness. It assures us that His Rest is not contingent on circumstances but is a constant source of comfort.

CHAPTER 8:

Rest in Our Daily Life

It is important for every believer to understand this Rest to which our Lord Jesus Christ has brought us back, to enjoy all the blessings God had for mankind from the beginning. Today children of God are not able to enjoy the blessings of God because they do not understand the true meaning of Rest; I do not intend to say that God has withheld his blessings. God will not stop his blessing for any reason, even at times you fall when you are in Christ, but it is possible that, though we have the blessings of God on us, we may still not be able to own the blessings of God in our lives just because we stay away from that Rest.

Clear sight but still searching

You may say, "Wait, wait! You have just completed explaining with all the scriptures saying that God, by His wisdom, brought us into this Rest...and now you say, though we are yet believers, we will not be able to own or enjoy God's blessing in our lives because we are not in His Rest. Are you contradicting what you have said earlier?" No! Let me explain with an example. One of my good friends who uses contact lenses once lost her lens after washing her face. She started searching for some time and could not find it. She asked her husband to help her find the lens, and both searched for quite some time but could not find it anywhere. Then her husband said not to worry, and they would get another set. After some time, she felt she could still see things very clearly. She then took a mirror and checked; the contact lens was still on her eye. This sounds very funny, doesn't it? It is possible that you might have also heard of such incidents around you.

But think about these questions.

- When my friend said that the lens was lost, was it really lost? *No!*
- Did she see clearly when she thought the lens was lost? *She did, but she did not realize that she saw clearly.*
- Did she enjoy the clear vision during the time she thought she lost the lens? *Though she had clear vision, she could not enjoy it, since her mind could not comprehend her clear vision; hence, she was looking for that lens.*

This is exactly what happens. When God has brought you into this Rest, He will never withdraw His Rest and His blessings from you. However, it is still possible that you will not be able to enjoy His blessings if you are not in His Rest while you are still inheriting that Rest. God has given you full control to enjoy Him when you are in Christ Jesus.

Many believers and even some Christian groups strongly believe in eternal Rest, which is very important, and I do not ignore the fact. But most believers lack the knowledge of God about the Rest which He brought to us as we are still in this world. While we talk about eternal Rest through the finished work of Jesus Christ, He also included spiritual Rest for our physical bodies. Physical Rest for our bodies through the typology of sleep and how sleep really helps our physical conditions forms an analogy of the promise of spiritual Rest for our natural bodies.

You may ask, "What is this spiritual Rest to our physical bodies?"

Philippians 4:7 (NKJV)

> *"...peace of God, which surpasses all understanding, will guard your hearts and minds through Christ Jesus."*

Walking in Rest still not enjoying

Can you really be at Rest when everything around you does not go as expected? It is very interesting to see how everyone perceives Rest. Many people think that they will only be at Rest when everything goes well around them. This may be true for the world without Jesus Christ, as they believe their Rest is defined by worldly circumstances. But for a believer, Rest comes from the Lord, surpassing all understanding. However, even for a believer, the choice to be at Rest remains.

God has graciously blessed me with a beautiful wife who has always been supportive in all that I do. I thank God for my wife, who is a wonderful beloved child of God. My wife became pregnant, and after a few years of marriage, she had to travel to the United States of America due to her job. After a difficult decision, we decided that she would travel first, and I would join her as soon as possible. However, after she left, I faced challenges in obtaining a visa through my company for various reasons. My boss, understanding my situation, showed me much favor and made significant efforts to secure my visa. Despite her best efforts, we were unsuccessful.

I eventually made the decision to quit my job

so that I could take care of my wife in the United States on a dependent visa. She was in a later stage of pregnancy, and I did not want her to travel back alone during that time. By God's grace, I found favor in my manager's eyes once again, and she suggested that I go on sabbatical leave. At first, I didn't see the purpose of taking sabbatical leave at that time, but I followed her advice as I felt a sense of peace. Consequently, I joined my wife.

Now, we encountered another challenging phase. During the delivery stages, my wife had to take a leave from work, which meant we only had half of her salary to rely on while also needing to cover the costs of the delivery and our living expenses. This situation was very difficult. I began searching for a job after obtaining my employment authorization document. However, finding a job in the United States with limited experience proved to be a challenge, leading to feelings of anxiety, stress, and emotional turmoil. My wife continued to encourage me, assuring me that everything would work together for our good. Despite knowing the truth in her words, I struggled to find Rest. I eventually fell into a state of depression and, regrettably, began causing difficulties for my wife instead of supporting her. I was fully aware of my wrong actions but couldn't seem to break free from them. I felt as though God was speaking to me deep within, assuring me that He had everything under control. However, I chose to focus on external circumstances rather than listening to the voice within me, which kept me in a state of anxiety.

Then something remarkable happened. My wife began experiencing labor pains and was admitted to the hospital, where she gave birth to our wonderful son at 10:30 pm. We were overjoyed and thanked God for our precious child. Another miracle unfolded at 11:30 pm when my manager from the company where I was on sabbatical leave, which was located on the other side of the globe, called me. They informed me about a job opening in the same country and city where I had come to be with my wife. This was truly an amazing work of God.

After this, I realized that the entire process of anxiety, pain, and depression, along with my choice not to find Rest and my contribution to an unpleasant atmosphere at home, was entirely my own choice. I could have chosen to be at Rest, and in doing so, I would have been able to fully enjoy the days of my wife's pregnancy—a true blessing from God. Unfortunately, I missed out on that blessing due to my choices. Could I have found Rest? Absolutely. This is how a believer sets themselves apart from the people of the world. Instead of focusing on problems in their situations, they learn to see Christ in every circumstance and enter into that Rest which our Lord has provided. This is why the scripture encourages us to make every effort to enter that Rest. Choosing to be in that spiritual Rest, relying on the inner voice of the Holy Spirit of God, enables you to enjoy all the fruits of the Spirit.

Rest is not an encouragement to lead a lazy life. Having work to do is a blessing, but performing that work from within the inner Rest is the true blessing. In this state, you are not only blessed but also become a blessing to those around you. When we read the scriptures in the book of Genesis, we see that God created all things, including mankind, in six days. On the seventh day, God brought everything He had created into His Rest and sanctified it. This portion of the scripture helps us understand that anything we do should be done from the Rest that God has brought us into through His blessing.

How to see Rest from its beginning

In a timeless realm beyond the confines of Earth, there existed a magnificent Garden of God. Within this garden, life thrived in harmony, and the very air was imbued with tranquility. At its heart stood the Eternal Fellowship in Rest, a symbol of the restful order that prevailed throughout creation.

Long ago, when the universe was but a canvas of possibilities, the Creator, our Father God, in all His wisdom, fashioned the Garden of God as a sanctuary of peace and perfection. It was a place where the melody of life's rhythms danced in unison, where the laughter of the streams and the whispers of the leaves blended seamlessly into a symphony of God.

As time unfolded, the Creator shaped humanity, bestowing upon them the precious gift of free will. With the freedom to choose, the first man and woman, Adam and Eve, were placed within the Garden. They basked in the radiance of the Tree of life, for its fruit held the essence of divine restfulness.

Yet, within this perfect realm, a whisper of temptation stirred a serpent, cunning and charming. It tempted Adam and Eve to taste the fruit of Knowledge, to grasp the understanding of good and evil. Their choice, driven by curiosity and desire, marked the turning point.

Upon partaking of the forbidden fruit, a veil of

uncertainty descended upon humanity. No longer could they simply Rest in the Creator's perfect order. The harmony of the Garden wavered, and the Tree of Life seemed distant, obscured by the shadow of newfound knowledge.

The consequence of their choice was evident. As they left the Garden, humanity entered a world where Rest became elusive, obscured by toil and suffering. The rhythms of life, once a joyous melody, now carried the dissonance of trials and tribulations.

Generations passed, and the memory of the Garden faded. Humanity toiled ceaselessly, seeking Rest through their own endeavors. Yet, the yearning for the Rest they once knew persisted, deep within their hearts.

In the fullness of time, a promise was whispered through the ages, a promise of restoration. The Creator, in His boundless love, devised a plan to reconcile humanity to the restful order they had forfeited. This plan, hidden in the depths of creation, awaited its moment of revelation.

One fateful night, beneath a sky ablaze with stars, a child was born in a humble manger. This child, Jesus, carried within Him the Tree of Life. His life would become a bridge between humanity's restless striving and the divine REST they longed for.

Through His teachings, His compassion, and His ultimate sacrifice, Jesus unveiled the path to Rest. He beckoned humanity to lay down their burdens, to find Rest for their souls, and to return to the harmonious rhythms of the Creator's design.

In the presence of Jesus, the weary found solace, the broken discovered healing, and the restless encountered true Rest. His life, a testament to divine love, offered the promise of eternal restfulness, an invitation to return to the Garden of God, to stand once more beneath the Tree of Life, in Jesus Christ.

As humanity embraced this promise, they began to realize that Rest was not merely a distant memory but a living reality, accessible through faith and trust. The rhythms of creation, once disrupted by choice, were restored through the grace of the Creator.

In the end, the Fellowship from Garden of God was not lost but found anew within the hearts of those who chose to believe. Humanity, once separated by their choices, had the opportunity to Rest in the embrace of their Creator's love, as they journeyed toward an eternal dawn of restful peace.

The story reminds us that even in the midst of life's trials and choices, the promise of Rest remains within our reach, waiting to be realized in our hearts.

While God offers us His Rest, He also honors our free will. He does not force us to accept or enjoy this Rest. Instead, He gives us the choice to embrace it or reject it. Our free will allows us to make decisions about how we respond to God's invitation and provision. Enjoying God's Rest is not automatic. It requires an intentional choice on our part. This choice involves:

Realization of Being Brought In: Recognizing that God has brought us into that Rest as a gift, and an act of His love can motivate us to embrace it more fully.

Daily Decision: Enjoying God's Rest is not a one-time decision but a daily one. We continually choose to Rest in God's love, care, and sovereignty, even in the midst of life's challenges.

Consequences of Choice: Our choice to enjoy or neglect God's Rest has consequences. Choosing to embrace His Rest leads to peace, joy, and spiritual growth. The only person who can keep you away from that Rest is YOU.

God's Unchanging Invitation: Even if we

momentarily fail to enjoy God's Rest due to our choices or circumstances, His invitation to Rest always remains open. He is a loving and patient God who always keeps you under the shadow of His Rest.

SUMMARY

In this series of passages, we've embarked on a profound journey that delves into the design of Rest, God's presence, and fellowship. These writings offer both personal reflections and in-depth explorations of spiritual truths.

At their core, these passages underscore the notion that Rest, whether it's of a spiritual or physical nature, is a cherished gift from God. They emphasize how faith and reliance on the Holy Spirit can bring about a deep sense of peace to see even life's most challenging moments from that Rest.

A central theme running through these writings is the idea that believers are temples of the Holy Spirit. This revelation serves as a powerful reminder that God's presence resides within us, and this inner dwelling is the source of genuine Rest and communion with our Creator.

Moreover, these passages highlight the heart of God, which yearns for fellowship with humanity. They convey that the giving of the Law, particularly the Ten Commandments, wasn't just a list of rules but a pathway to fellowship, rest, and righteousness—a gift bestowed through Christ's work. This righteousness allows us to enter into God's Rest and partake in a restored relationship with Him.

The discussion surrounding various feasts and holy days underscores their symbolic significance in drawing believers nearer to God and commemorating the redemptive work of Jesus Christ. They stress the importance of embracing Rest as a means to deepen our connection with the divine.

In summary, these passages encourage us to acknowledge and embrace the Rest that God offers and brought us into. They teach us to seek His presence and cherish the fellowship that He ardently desires to share with us. They remind us that through faith and the indwelling of the Holy Spirit, we can find Rest amidst life's trials, and in this Rest, we can experience the profound blessings of God's love and grace and understand the heart of our Creator.

END NOTES

Everyone in this world seeks to have peace in their inner man. In the journey we've taken through the pages of this book, we've explored from the scriptures the profound mystery of REST and it being given as a gift by our Lord, Jesus Christ. We've learned that our Father God gave us His only begotten and beloved Son, even to the death of the cross, to bring us into this Rest; it is a way of living, a lens through which we can experience God's fullness.

As we conclude, let's take a moment to reflect on the key insights we've gathered. Rest is not about earning it or struggling to enter into it but, rather, knowing that Jesus Christ brought us into it freely, and we are expected to be in it and enjoin the fellowship of GOD.

In our fast-paced lives, we often find ourselves rushing from one task to another, our minds racing ahead of us. Being at Rest both physically and spiritually teaches us to slow down, to savor each experience, and to be fully aware of our thoughts, emotions, and sensations. It's a powerful tool for reducing stress, enhancing focus, and cultivating a sense of inner peace.

But Rest isn't just about laziness; it's about our

state of mind. By being at Rest, we learn to enjoy the fellowship of GOD and with others. We become better beings and are better able to start looking at others as God sees them. The ripple effects of being at Rest extend far beyond ourselves, touching the lives of those around us.

As we move forward from this book, remember that being at Rest, to which our Lord has brought us back, is not a destination but a lifelong journey. There will be days when it's easy and days when it's challenging. The key is to approach each day with an open heart and a willingness to embrace whatever arises with the eyes of Christ. Just as a river flows around obstacles, our mindfulness can help us navigate the challenges of life with grace and resilience.

Thank you for embarking on this journey of Rest, God's design for mankind, with me. May your days be filled with Rest, presence, gratitude, and an unwavering connection to the beauty that surrounds you.

ABOUT THE AUTHOR

Satish Mylapore is a debut author but a strong believer of inner truths. With a lifelong dedication to exploring the realms of understanding the Father's heart, Satish has emerged as a trusted voice in the realm of personal transformation and spiritual awakening.

Drawing from his background in spiritual insights, Satish's journey has taken him from traditional to insightful meditations. His deep immersion in meditation, mindfulness, and mysticism has allowed him to distill timeless wisdom into accessible and spiritual teachings for the earnest seeker.

Satish's personal experience with God laid the foundation for his in-depth study of spiritual systems. However, it was his thirst that ignited his passion for sharing the profound insights he has gained on his path.

In addition to his role as an emerging author, he works in the Information Technology Industry. He believes that spirituality is not confined to temples or rituals but is a way of living authentically and with intention. He is a proponent of blending spiritual principles with everyday experiences to create a life imbued with meaning, love, compassion, and gratitude reflecting Jesus Christ on earth.

When he's not writing or guiding others on their spiritual journey, Satish enjoys spending time with his beautiful wife Sathya Priya, his two children Josiah and Josana, engaging in soul-enriching conversations. He invites you to connect with his email satish.mylapore@gmail.com.

Satish's mission is to enable individuals to uncover their own spiritual truths, enjoy God as a Father even on this earth with you still having breath in the nostril, foster inner harmony, and radiate love and light into the world.

Printed in the USA
CPSIA information can be obtained
at www.ICGtesting.com
LVHW021116051024
792970LV00017B/1060

9 798893 334265